Breaking the Curse

I0027242

Charlotte Russell Johnson

The Curse

These things keep lingering
They're lingering over my life
They didn't happen once
They happened at least twice

These things they keep lingering
They're lingering in mind
They didn't hurt me just once
It happened at least twice

This pain keeps lingering
It's lingering in my soul
It wasn't pain just once
It was pain at least twice

The damage keeps lingering
It's lingering over my life
It wasn't damage just once
It was damage at least twice

This curse keeps lingering
It's lingering in my family
It didn't curse just once
It cursed at least twice

Victory is lingering
It's coming to my life
It's not coming just once
It's coming for life!

This curse is no longer lingering
It's no longer in my family
It wasn't broken just once
It was broken for life!

Dedication

This book is dedicated to the littlest victim as you make your transformation from victim to overcomer.

Selah!!!

In Memory

of

Wallace 'Maurice' Russell

August 25, 1939 - May 17, 2009

You will always be a part of me.

THE CURSE BROKEN

Preface 9

Introduction 13

My Daddy 17

Planting Seeds 21

Daddy's Hugs 51

Water 63

I've Seen it All 65

It Happened to me! 79

Tell Me 93

Who are These Molesters 95

It's Easier to Hide 107

No Harm... No Offense 117

Secrets, Secrets 129

Tattletale 141

Assumption Junction 155

Useless Excuses 161

Sacrificial Lamb 169

Scapegoat 175

Dreams, Hopes, Wishes 185

If Only 187

Decent Decency 191

Black Sheep, Black Sheep 203

Green With Envy 217

Bitter Victory 225

Victory 229

Additional Information 235

Preface

Delinquency, youth violence, gangs, early sexual involvement, alcohol and drug abuse and other problem behaviors in our young people are causes for grave concern in our society. Throughout recorded history, concern for the values and morals of young people was an enduring adult preoccupation. This worry includes a concern for the character of future generations. The concern, however, has never been enough to ensure that the children possess the type of character that can sustain the individual and society.

Many values and principles will weaken as they are passed on from one generation to the next. Still, other parents will fail to understand the seriousness of the responsibility that God has entrusted to them. Parenting is an awesome responsibility that cannot be taken lightly or irrelevantly.

An old cliché says, "A chain is only as strong as its weakest link." If this theory holds true, then a family or society is only as strong as its weakest link. If we were to look at the various components that make up our society and refer to them as links, we would see that one of the most vital links in that chain is the children. I submit that if the children can be destroyed or weakened, society as a whole becomes weaker. If Satan succeeds in destroying the children, then society as we know it will be destroyed, also.

Within each family, there are generational secrets. These secrets are so deep that sometimes it is almost impossible to discover their root or origin. Many of these are generational curses. I submit to you that a family is no stronger than its weakest curse. My desire in writing this book is to address those hidden demons that seek to destroy our offsprings and our descendants.

God structured the family unit in the same fashion that He structured the relationship of the church to Christ. God instituted the family structure. The family is a vital link in the chain that makes a solid society. I have decided to take a stand for Christ. It's time to break the curse.

This book is also a deviation from those in the *A Journey to Hell and Back* sequence. The books in that series include A *Journey to Hell and Back, The Flip Side, Grace Under Fire: The Journey Never Ends*, and *Mama May I*. My second book, *Daddy's Hugs* and my sixth book, *In the Lord's Eyes: Mama's Pearls* are also distinct from the series. For my loyal fans, I will eventually write the next book in that sequence. There are many more stories yet to be told.

Disclaimer:

Many of the names in this book have been changed and significant descriptive details have been omitted. Any perceived reference to people that you may know is merely coincidental.

All scripture references are from the King James Bible unless otherwise noted.

Breaking the Curse

*The disciples were meeting
behind locked doors because
they were afraid of the Jewish
leaders. Suddenly, Jesus was
standing there among them!*
John 20:19 NLT

_____Introduction by Earline Hall

Breaking the Curse is the seventh book in author Charlotte Johnson's series of motivational works. This book explores the complex relationships and dynamics involved in functional and dysfunctional families. Once again, Ms. Johnson addresses the problems within families by using real life examples. Ms. Johnson deals with revealing family secrets and their impact. Readers of Ms. Johnson's earlier books are familiar with her willingness to tackle difficult subjects in an informative and entertaining manner. *Breaking the Curse* has an increased level of poetic expression and symbolism when compared with her other books. The balance of family stories, poetry, and family pictures provide the reader with a feeling of connectedness to the family, inspiration, and humor.

Ms. Johnson uses her family experiences and the experiences of others to illustrate the destructive nature of family secrets. She reveals intimate and scandalous family secrets in order to help others and prevent harm to others. *Breaking the Curse* will shock and touch the hearts of many generations with its intimate and extremely personal accounts of childhood experiences reminiscent of Alice Walker's *The Color Purple, A Child Called It,* and *A Bastard Out of North Carolina.*

Poems such as *Scapegoat, Sacrificial Lamb, Secrets, Secrets, Green with Envy, It Happened to Me,* and *Useless Excuses* grab the reader's attention and give insight into the feelings of people as they perform their roles within the family. The poems give voice to the experiences of families. Each chapter begins with a poem to foreshadow the story that is about to be told.

This book offers hope to those who have experienced pain, disillusionments, heartaches, suffering, and abandonment. Revealing secrets, dealing with the ramifications of the revelation, and the consequences of actions help to promote growth and healing. Internal scars and wounds must be treated to prevent past hurts from killing future hope and progress. Ms. Johnson exhorts each of us to look inside of ourselves to ensure that we think not only of the safety and progress of our families, and ourselves but develops empathy and courage to fight sin, evil, and injustice to help others. Evil thrives when we repress our past or becomes apathetic and ambivalent to the suffering of others and do not have compassion for others who are in danger. *Breaking the Curse* encourages good people to educate themselves, be informed, and be willing to fight sin to ensure that "family curses" are broken and that future generations can experience a life that is not bound by past sins that have taken root, grown, and thrived in the roots of their family tree.

This book reminds us to show love, compassion, and concern for others who suffer. Each of us will one day need to be comforted. As a society, it has become easier to overlook injustice for the sake of convenience. *Breaking the Curse* reminds us that it is everyone's duty to be involved, to sacrifice in order to help others and prevent future harm to the innocent. This book is excellent for those who need encouragement, work with families, have suffered from hurt, disappointment, abuse, neglect and betrayal or who work with these populations. As the reader travels through this novel with Ms. Johnson into dark tunnels and even darker closets, hope is ever present as the journey gets closer to the light at the end of the tunnel.

My Daddy

By La'Toya Alexandria Hall

My daddy, he loved me.
His love held no end.
He adored me.
He was my first, my best, and my closest friend.

He helped to raise me when I was a little pup.
And when I fell out of trees, he bandaged me up.
As a little child, I was accident-prone.
But he'd fix me up, wipe my tears, and still let me
roam.
When I got banged up, he'd argue with my
grandma and my mommy.
His philosophy was to "just let the child be!"

He taught me to fight, just in case he wasn't free,
But he still wanted to be there to always protect me.
He fought my battles. He tackled 'em all.
He taught me that I should always and forever
stand tall.

My daddy was a busy man; he had to go to work.
When my daddy walked out the door, I always felt
so hurt.
I could do not one thing
Because all my sunshine turned to rain
But then my daddy would come home again and
into his arms, I'd spring.

My daddy used to walk with me.
My daddy used to talk with me.
My daddy always sparred with me.
My daddy never could beat me.

But then one day, I had to set this daddy free,
Because he wasn't real, he was imaginary.
He was based on some other men that came into
my life,
Some that loved the women in my life, and one
that made my grandma his wife.

It was also based on my uncle who I loved more
than life.
He was my friend, my confidante, and my partner
in crime.

He taught me many languages like how to speak in mime.

He taught me a love for music, which he considers to be his wife.

He taught me how to sing, how to rap, and words that cut like a knife.

Because we shared these gifts, we'll be tight for life.

But I never found a perfect daddy, and an imaginary one wouldn't do.

So I looked into the book for a love that's tried and true.

It was the love of my real heavenly father.

I found the love of God.

He's here to love you, too.

Now, I've found a love that I know is true.

Now, what about you?

Have you done what you need to do?

Herman Alexander Hall

Planting Seeds

Wherein in time past ye walked according to the course of this world, according to the prince of the power of the air, the spirit that now worketh in the children of disobedience:
Ephesians 2:2

Lil' Earline

Our lives are filled with expectations. There are things that we expect of others. There are things that are expected from us. Some expectations will be fulfilled by the expected source. Some expectations will be fulfilled by unexpected sources. Other expectations will be fulfilled at unexpected times.

During the early years of our lives, we often find fault with the parenting and nurturing skills of those entrusted with our care. We have a better answer for every problem. We have a better way of getting each task accomplished. We promise ourselves that we will be much better parents. At some point, all of the promises of our youth are tested. All the seeds that we have sown will spring up. Seeds of rebellion, discontent, ingratitude, stubbornness, and countless others will appear at a time when we are not expecting them.

On October 2, 1974, at age 15, my first pregnancy resulted in the birth of an 8 pounds 5 ounces baby girl, Earline. My daughter was the only child, only grandchild, only great grandchild, and the only great-great-grandchild. At the age of five, she had committed her life to God. At age seven, she began to pray for a miracle. Earline was lonely and tired of being the only child. She prayed her mother would become pregnant. Her prayer request was granted. What seemed impossible to man was a simple request for God.

> *Behold, children are a gift of the LORD; The fruit of the womb is a reward. Like arrows in the hand of a warrior; So are the children of one's youth. How blessed is the man whose quiver is full of them; They shall not be ashamed, When they speak with their enemies in the gate.*
> Psalms 127:3-5

My son, Herman, is as special as his conception. He was always very active, rough, adventurous, or shall we just say, "All boy." His time inside my womb should have given me an indication of what to expect from the child. He was exceptional from the very beginning. During the pregnancy, there was constant moving and kicking.

During the latter months of the pregnancy, it seemed a one-man football game was going on inside of me. The skin on my stomach was extremely tight. It seemed impossible that it would stretch to accommodate the pregnancy. Herman seemed determined to expand his tight quarters. As I looked at my stomach, it would often appear that a fist was protruding from it. In the end, my skin did stretch. The stretching wasn't confined to my stomach. The tight skin that was covering other areas of my body began to relax.

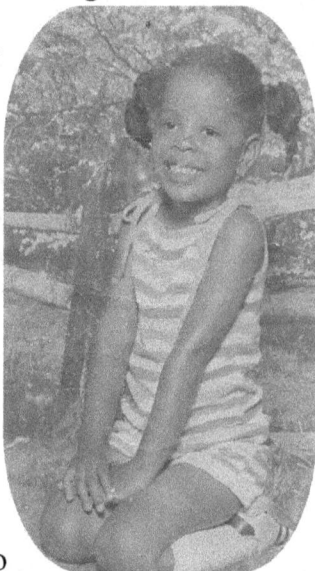

My pregnancy with Earline had been an easy one. I expected the same from Herman. With Earline, I was in labor for less than an hour. She was born without excessive pain. There was no need for a pain medication. I assumed things would go very similarly with Herman. I was wrong.

Herman's expected due date was in early January. I reasoned that it would be better if he were born a couple of weeks early. If he was born on Christmas, we would be able to celebrate his birthday and Christmas together. This was my excuse for being impatient. Anxious to help God with the process, I asked my great-grandmother (Mae) how I could induce my labor. She advised me that if I took a dose of castor oil my contractions would start. The taste was horrible and I didn't swallow much of it. After a few hours at the hospital, I was sent home.

A few days later, I had another bright idea. Wouldn't it be nice to have the first baby born on New Year's Day? As the day passed, I became more anxious. As much as I hated the taste of the castor oil, I decided to try it again. This time, Mae told me to chase it with some lemon juice. The lemon juice didn't kill the taste. It took several attempts before I got enough of the horrible concoction in my system. New Year's Day had passed. Later that day, January 2, 1983, I began to have cramps. They weren't contractions. Nevertheless, I was hopeful the discomfort would lead to real contractions. We made the second trip to the hospital. The next morning, I woke up and was shocked to learn that I was still pregnant. This time, I was almost mad. I drank that mess for nothing.

*O Lord, I will praise Thee:
though Thou wast angry with
me, Thine anger is turned away,
and Thou comfortedst me.
Behold, God is my salvation; I*

*will trust, and not be afraid: for
the Lord JEHOVAH is my
strength and my song; He also is
become my salvation.*
Isaiah 12:1-2

When the doctor made his rounds, I begged him to induce my labor. He didn't know about my own feeble attempts. He ordered something to help me. The real contractions started for a while. They were mild and soon began to fade. When the doctor checked on me the second time, he asked me if I would need anything for the pain. Based on my professional opinion and previous experience, I assured him that I was capable of delivering my baby without pain medication. After all, I had done it before. This time, he administered the medicine to help my labor. As he left the room, he turned back to offer some final words of concern.

Almost knowingly, he said, "If you change your mind about the pain medication let me know."

Before he made his way down the hall, I was screaming as loud as I could, "COME BACK!"

That was the last thing that I remembered before waking up, and being told that my son was born healthy. When I asked if I was alert during his birth, I

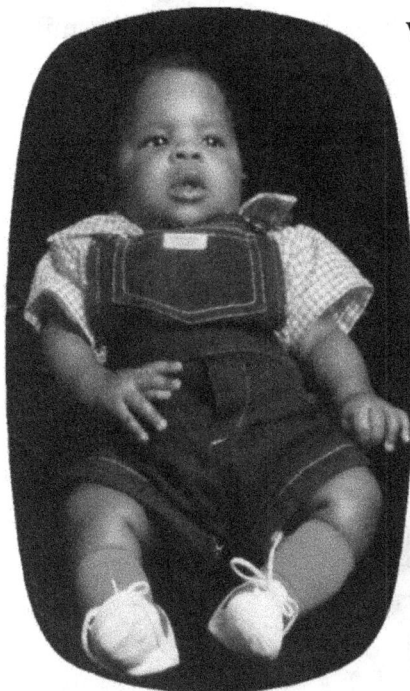

was told that I was. The pain was apparently more than I wanted to remember. On January 3, 1983, after twenty-three hours of labor, I gave birth to a healthy baby boy, Herman Alexander Hall. He was named after my father and my grandmother. This was my miracle baby!

Miraculously, my body survived the pregnancy with relative ease. Beyond that, the pregnancy had actually aided my body in the recovery process. We never forgot that he was a miracle. He gave us many reminders. I had many expectations from Herman. What I got wasn't exactly what I was expecting.

Herman is warm and sensitive, and he idolizes his older sister, Earline. As a young child, he began to make friends easily. Whenever we would go to a store, he would make at least one new friend before leaving. His friends are not restricted by age, race, or socioeconomic status. Nevertheless, he wasn't like the mild-mannered reserved Earline. He was strong-willed and was determined to do things his own way. Herman is also friendly, energetic, charming, and personable. The problem with his behavior was that his way of doing things was usually my wrong way. This child inherited all my excess baggage and many of my bad habits. At the time, I didn't know what was wrong with Herman. I was desperate to change his behavior.

Foolishness is bound up in the heart of a child but the rod of correction will drive it far from him.
Proverbs 22:15

My attempts to correct Herman's behavior often seemed futile. Only, it took years for me to realize what was at the root of the problem. There were many times that I was frustrated to the point of giving up. Earline became a type of second mother to him. She waged her own war to correct his behavior. Years later, my granddaughter La'Toya would become his third mother.

When Herman was almost seven-months-old, I placed him on the living room floor on top of a blanket. I went outside to hang up clothes on the clothes' line. When I returned inside of the house, he was standing up at the living room table. A week later, Herman began walking. By the time he was a year old, he had a very large vocabulary of words. In addition, by the time he was eighteen-months-old, he could easily carry on an intelligible conversation. Early on, Herman developed one habit. This habit would be very hard for him to break. He preferred to slip off from home, rather than ask for permission. Now, after carefully observing my mother's behavior, I'm convinced that he inherited this habit from her.

When he was a toddler, Herman spent a lot of time with my Uncle Teddy. Teddy liked to take Herman for long walks. Herman was short for his age, and he walked at seven months. These two factors together made him irresistible to women. Teddy used Herman to perfect his game. He used him to collect telephone numbers. Whenever Herman was with him, women stopped.

They remarked, "Ooh! He's so cute."

This gave my uncle a chance to ask for their telephone numbers. He was also teaching the child to repeat this behavior.

If there be therefore any consolation in Christ, if any comfort of love, if any fellowship of the Spirit, if any bowels and mercies, Fulfil ye my joy, that ye be likeminded, having the same love, being of one accord, of one mind. Let nothing be done through strife or vainglory but in lowliness of mind let each esteem other better than themselves. Look not every man on his own things but every man also of the things of others.
Philippians 2:1-4

Herman knew everyone in the neighborhood who woke up early in the mornings and everyone who drank coffee. Herman loved coffee, which I seldom made. He got his love for coffee from my grandmother,

Ma'Dear. Most of her children and grandchildren love coffee. This love was not passed on to me. When Herman was about a year old, this habit got him in trouble.

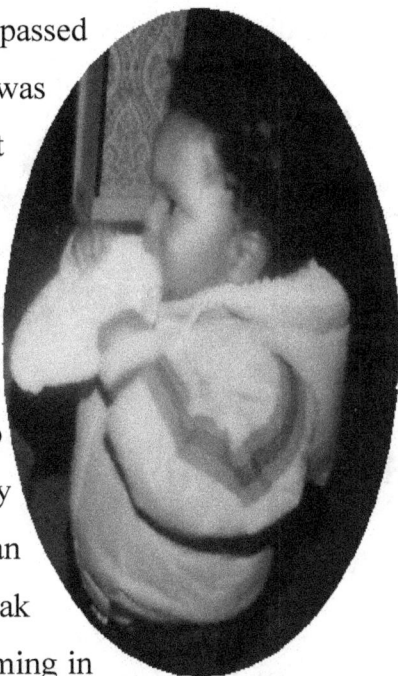

Upon arriving home one night, he requested a cup of coffee. The weather was cold, so I decided to immediately prepare the coffee. Herman stopped next door to speak to our neighbor before coming in the house.

After I prepared the cup of coffee, I placed it on the washing machine. Herman ran in the house. As I was getting him an ice cube from the freezer to cool the coffee, he grabbed the cup of coffee. He turned the cup over before I could stop him. Herman's wrist was burned but the jacket that he was wearing protected him from extensive injury. He was never big on crying, and this would be no exception. This may also have been because Earline was crying and screaming hysterically.

She cried repeatedly, "Oh God, don't let my brother die! This is my only brother!"

She screamed this all the way to the hospital. Perhaps, she was having a flashback to the time when I had been burned. When we arrived at the hospital, the nurse made an excuse to send me back to the front desk. This was to allow her time to question Earline about Herman's accident. When she asked Earline what had happened to Herman, Earline understood the implications and responded.

Annoyed she responded, "Ask him! He can talk!"

Herman explained to the nurse how he had been burned. When I walked back into the room, the nurse was finishing her questions.

She said to him, "I bet you don't want any more coffee!"

To this statement, he responded, "I'm going to get me a cup as soon as I get home!"

I am the LORD, and there is none else, there is no God beside Me: I girded thee, though thou hast not known Me: That they may know from the rising of the sun, and from the west, that there is none beside Me. I am the LORD, and there is none else.
Isaiah 45:5-6

During his early years, it was necessary for us to make several trips to the hospital emergency room. He was always getting into something. When he was around four years old, I noticed that his pinkie finger was crooked on his right hand. It was also slightly swollen. This was obviously not the normal condition of his finger. As a concerned and dutiful mother, I began to question him. Upset I asked, "Herman what happened to your finger!?"

He responded calmly, "Oh! I hurt it the other day playing football."

Still confused, I probed further, "Who were you playing with?"

Reluctant to give me further details, he added, "Buck Daddy and Uncle Teddy."

Determined to get the answers that I needed, I pressed for understanding, "Tell me what happened!"

He answered just as determined, "When I caught the ball, my finger went back."

Still confused, I asked, "Where was I when this happened? I don't remember hearing you cry."

He responded simply, "You were in the house but I didn't cry."

Confused, even more, I continued, "You didn't cry! Well, did it hurt!?'

He answered as if he was becoming irritated, "Yes! But I didn't cry!"

Becoming more agitated and confused, I asked, "Why!?"

He stated simply, "They said, 'real men don't cry.'"

We took Herman to the hospital emergency room. The x-rays revealed that the bones of his broken finger had begun to grow back together in the deformed pattern. If we wanted the finger to heal correctly, the bone would have to be broken and reset. We decided against re-breaking his finger. Like a "Real Man," he didn't cry but the damage remains.

I will continue this everlasting covenant between us, generation after generation. It will continue between me and your offspring forever. And I will always be

*your God and the God of your
descendants after you.*
Genesis 17:7 NLT

Herman attended a daycare center in downtown Columbus. Each morning, it was necessary for me to drive him to school. Each morning, in route to the daycare, we stopped by Ma'Dear's house. Whenever the grandchildren came by her house, Ma'Dear always had something to give the children. Herman had a bad habit of jumping out the car wherever it stopped. On this morning, I caught him before he was able to get out of the car. After we left Ma'Dear's house, we drove towards the Thirteenth Street Bridge. Below this bridge were numerous train tracks. There was a low wall (maybe less than two feet high) that served as the only barrier along the bridge to prevent you from falling off the bridge, and down onto the train track. This wasn't much of a barrier. If you staggered too close to the edge, you could easily fall off the bridge.

The traffic was always heavy on weekdays around this time of the morning. When I turned left onto the bridge, the car door swung open on Herman's side of the car. At the time, Herman was four years old. He was holding onto the door and bouncing up and down.

He had opened the door at Ma'Dear's house. In his effort to hide this from me, Herman held onto the inside door handle.

Cars were coming up the road behind me. Cars were also coming from the opposite direction. I was afraid to stop too fast because I feared that his grip would be broken or that someone would hit me from behind. I eased the car to a stop. Calmly, he climbed back into the car. When we arrived at the school, I checked him carefully to be sure that he wasn't hurt. During the ordeal, Herman never cried, and made only one statement.

He calmly stated, "My shoestrings broke."

He was wearing new tennis shoes. The torn shoestrings were the only visible signs of this ordeal. When I told Mama what had happened to him, she said during the night she had a strong urge to pray.

"I started to pray lying in the bed but I could tell that God wanted me to get on my knees. I obeyed and got down on my knees and began to pray. I'm glad that I obeyed."

Herman never stopped jumping out of the car. This was just one of his many adventures. As the years

38

passed, he became more adventurous.

> *Blessed are the undefiled in the way, who walk in the law of the LORD. Blessed are they that keep His testimonies, and that seek Him with the whole heart.*
> Psalm 119:1-2

Herman had confessed salvation at age five, and the devil had fought him from that point on.

Mama said to God one day, "Lord, you have blessed me to witness to a lot of people but I have never seen any of them get *saved*."

A few days later, on a Sunday morning, she walked into her bedroom and found Herman. He was on his knees leaning over the red velvet stool at the foot of the bed. He was engrossed in prayer. He never heard Mama enter the room. Herman had been listening to Jimmy Swaggart on television. When the preacher made the call for salvation, Herman accepted the call.

When Mama came back into the room, she questioned Herman.

With excited anticipation, Mama asked, "Herman, what were you doing!? Were you praying!?"

He said simply, "Yes Ma'am."

She continued, "Were you saying what Jimmy Swaggart was saying on TV?"

Again, he responded, "Yes Ma'am."

Overjoyed, Mama exclaimed, "Herman, you're *saved*! You're not only my grandson; you're my brother in the Lord!"

> *If we are unfaithful, He remains faithful, for He cannot deny who He is.*
> 2 Timothy 2:13 NLT

A battle ensued from that point on. There were constant mishaps or accidents. The devil was unwilling to give up on Herman. There were times that I was tempted to give up.

One night, we were headed to church. We stopped at a nearby gas station, and I went in to pay for the gas. Everyone else had supposedly remained in the car. After I pumped the gas, we headed across town to my uncle's home. When we arrived, someone asked about Herman. We had no idea what had happened to him. We rushed back to the gas station. Herman was sitting calmly on the curb. After giving him a verbal reprimand, we headed to a store near the church. Again, everyone was supposed to stay in the car. After purchasing a couple of items, I returned to the car. Thinking that everyone was accounted for, I drove on to the church.

The church was about five minutes away. Upon our arrival at the church, we each sat in our customary seats. Shortly after our arrival, someone handed me Herman's Bible. When I turned to give it to him, he wasn't in his seat. I questioned my mother and Earline about his location. Once again, he had jumped out of the car. They had assumed that I knew this information or that I had seen Herman in the relatively small store. I hadn't. They hadn't noticed that he didn't come out of the store with me. I rushed back to the store, arriving just before they closed for the evening. Herman was walking around the toy department. He hadn't noticed our departure.

And since it is through God's kindness, then it is not by their good works. For in that case, God's grace would not be what it really is—free and undeserved Romans 11:6 NLT

When he was around five years old, he was

supposed to be playing outside in the yard. When it started getting dark, I began looking for him. Earline and I walked around the nearby trailers calling his name. He didn't respond. We questioned all of his friends. No one knew what had happened to him. We were forced to call the police. The officer walked around the trailers shining his flashlight beneath them. Herman was found beneath one of them. He was asleep.

As Herman grew older, his escapades accelerated, almost beyond my ability to endure them. If I was expecting him to be a mild-mannered childlike Earline, I was sadly mistaken. I tried to be his mother, father, and reformer.

When we think of a rod, we usually think of a physical or literal rod, i.e., a belt, switch, or strap. I tried using these with Herman, to no avail. All the traditional methods and many nontraditional methods of discipline failed. He refused to cry and repeated his behavior. He was always extremely courteous and likable. However, he was a force to be reckoned with when he felt challenged, crossed or threatened. Finally, after one of his escapades, I figured out what the real problem was.

Blessed is the man that walketh

42

> *not in the counsel of the
> ungodly, nor standeth in the way
> of sinners, nor sitteth in the seat
> of the scornful. But his delight is
> in the law of the LORD, and in
> His law doth he meditate day
> and night. And he shall be like a
> tree planted by the rivers of
> water, that bringeth forth his
> fruit in his season, his leaf also
> shall not wither, and whatsoever
> he doeth shall prosper.*
> Psalm 1:1-3

The seeds of disobedience that I sowed had to be reaped, although my daughter says 'the reaping' really wasn't that bad. That's because she wasn't the one receiving the reaping. The reaping was extremely painful. Knowing that I caused my own pain intensified the pain. Herman picked up many of my habits, good and bad.

There were constant calls from the schools about things that he was doing there. He did very little to apply himself academically. My efforts to refine his behavior were unsuccessful. My love for marijuana was passed on to him. Many times, it appeared that he hated me. He refused to come home at any decent hour. His friends were the ones that break a mother's heart. It would have been easier if I could have said he was just like his father but I refused to speak this curse over his life. In actuality, he's just like his mother.

When we moved into our house, he developed another trick. He took one of my lawn chairs and placed it at the edge of the fence in the backyard. He placed another chair on the opposite side of the fence. This was to help him make a speedy escape when he needed to jump the fence. To correct this problem, I added barbwire to the fence. This didn't stop him.

> *Love each other with genuine*
> *affection, and take delight in*
> *honoring each other.*
> Romans 12:10 NLT

My mother has a love for oriental rugs. One Saturday afternoon, she was nagging me about taking her to purchase one of these rugs. Rather than doing this, I stopped to have my nails done. Not to be thwarted, she continued whining about the rug. This is just her way of getting her way. Finally, I told her that if she weren't afraid, she would let Herman take her to pick up the rug. This was supposed to be a joke, because Herman had never driven a car on the road. Actually, he had only pulled a car into the driveway. At the time, he was about fifteen-years-old.

Herman asked me to give him the keys to the car. Still thinking that we were joking, I gave them to him. Mama went out the door with him and got into the car. In my thoughts, surely, he wouldn't drive off in my car. To my utter dismay, Herman drove the car onto one of the busiest streets in Columbus. Mama had been driving for years but was afraid to drive on this street.

Mama said that when she told Herman to stop at the red light, he responded, "I've never done that."

O taste and see that the LORD is good: blessed is the man that trusteth in Him.
Psalm 34:8

They made it safely to the store but Mama was realizing the danger that surrounded them. She told Herman to tell me to come pick her up because she wasn't riding back to the nail salon with him. Mama was so scared that she had forgotten that she could drive. Realizing he was scared, too, reluctantly, she got back into the car. Herman was still behind the steering wheel. Mama prayed all the way back to the store.

When they returned to the nail salon, Herman asked, "Where do you want me to park?"

Relieved that they had made it back safely, Mama responded, "Anywhere!"

This experience caused me to look at Herman differently. If challenged, this was something that I would have done. After all, his mother taught herself to drive. The problem was that he was just like me. He had inherited most of my bad habits and all of my good habits.

Wrestling with Herman's behavior was like wrestling with me. I realized that he was my child, and as such, he needed lots of love. He needed to be accepted for who he was. I stopped trying to change him and started working on accepting him. I needed a special rod of correction for him. This didn't mean that I liked the behavior. It didn't mean that I stopped fussing. It simply meant that I had a better understanding of what I was facing. The traditional methods of discipline hadn't worked with me, and they weren't working with him. Verbally, I said he was changing. My words began to speak blessings into his life.

Remember, O LORD, Thy tender

46

*mercies and Thy
lovingkindnesses; for they have
been ever of old. Remember not
the sins of my youth, nor my
transgressions: according to Thy
mercy remember Thou me for
Thy goodness' sake, O LORD.*
Psalm 25:6-7

A couple of months after the driving incident, Herman got into trouble at school, and I made a desperate decision to pull him out of school. He was in the ninth grade and showing no efforts to pass on to the tenth grade. The school district wanted to send him to the alternative school. I informed them that Herman wouldn't be returning to public school. A month later, I was prepared to send him off to the Job Corps in North Carolina.

Not wanting to go, Herman said, "Mama I want to go back to school!"

As I looked into the eyes of my baby, I almost changed my decision but I was resolved to do what was best for him.

Resolutely, I told him, "You are my child but you don't have to make my mistakes."

This was the turning point for both of us. Rather

than getting frustrated with his behavior, I began to deal with him the way I dealt with myself. Talking to him and punishing him wasn't going to work; he would have to learn from his own mistakes.

Herman arrived safely at the Job Corps, in spite of several adventures that he took during the extended bus trip. He wasn't prone to go directly anywhere. Each time the bus would stop, he went exploring his surroundings. The week that he arrived at Job Corps, he went through diagnostic testing. He only missed one question on all of his tests. The next week, he passed the GED exam. Immediately, I began arranging for him to come home to take the SAT.

On his first weekend pass, I took him to a college in Atlanta where he made 1000 on the SAT. This was remarkable, since, he had never given any effort to learning anything, and he hadn't completed the ninth grade. Within a month, Herman started college.

When Herman went off to college at sixteen, what did he do? He assumed that his sole purpose in being there was to collect telephone numbers. Actually, he started collecting numbers before he started college. Numbers were on paper plates, fast-food wrappers, paper bags, on the closet walls, and anything else that he found handy. I wonder where he learned this habit – Uncle Teddy.

> *Don't let anyone capture you with empty philosophies and high-sounding nonsense that come from human thinking and from the spiritual powers of this world, rather than from Christ. For in Christ lives all the fullness of God in a human body.*
> Colossians 2:8-9

After a few months, I brought him back to Columbus. This was when the biggest battle for his soul took place. As God began to draw Herman, the devil began to fight to keep him. I was determined that he would not destroy my child. The devil seemed just as determined to destroy him. Herman offered little resistance to his tactics. In the heat of the battle, we began to leave the radios in the house tuned to Christian stations twenty-four hours a day. We saturated the house with the Word and praise. To this curse that still seeks to destroy him, I speak now!

You have no place in his life. Your influence has been canceled. This child was dedicated and consecrated to God. He has a purpose and mission in life to fulfill his God-ordained destiny. He will fulfill that purpose and you will not hinder him. He is the chosen seed of God. He is part of a royal priesthood and a holy generation. Everything that you meant for bad in his life, God is going to use it for good. God is accomplishing the purpose for his life and you are not able to withstand the hand of God. He is walking above the circumstances in his life. Things are not as they appear. The hand of God is upon his life and no weapon that is formed against him shall prosper. Your assignment has been canceled. This seed and his seed after him will serve only The True and Living God. It is so in Jesus name!

Earline Hall

Daddy's Hugs

What exactly is it that you expect of me?
Please define it for me?
Is it something that I could never be?
Is it something that I don't know how to be?

A daughter to my mother!?
Is that what you expect me to be?
That's a bit confusing to me...
She's trying to be something she could never be...
A Mommy and a Daddy to me...
So what is it that you expect me to rise above?
I had no Daddy's hugs, no Daddy's kisses,
and no Daddy's love...

A mother to my child!?
Why would you expect that of me?
I've got my own issues, can't you see?
There is still a hole inside of me...
No one has defined a man's love for me...

I had no Daddy's hugs, no Daddy's kisses,
and no Daddy's love...

A father to my daughter!?
Did you really expect that of me?
Coddle her, hold her, reassure her...
Is that what you really expected from me?
Fondle her, molest her, and threaten her...
That's what it meant to me...
Who was my example supposed to be?
I had no Daddy's hugs, no Daddy's kisses,
and no Daddy's love...

A father to my son!?
How could you expect that of me?
That's the laughing one...
I still wonder where "Real Men" come from...
Who was supposed to teach that to me?
I had no Daddy's hugs, no Daddy's kisses,
and no Daddy's love...

A son to my mother!?

Is that what you expect from me?

Where was I supposed to learn that from?

Was she the one I was supposed to get my
masculinity from?

She confused me with all her sensitivity...

My Daddy, she could never be...

Who was the example to me?

I had no Daddy's hugs, no Daddy's kisses,
and no Daddy's love...

A wife to my husband!?

Is that something you really expected of me?

Honor him, respect him, and support him?

What's that supposed to mean to me?

I have only seen strong independent women...

I don't have that identity...

Who was supposed to teach that to me?

I had no Daddy's hugs, no Daddy's kisses,
and no Daddy's love...

A husband to my wife!?

Is that something you really expected of me?

Respect her, protect her, and be faithful to her...
What's that supposed to mean to me?
Neglect her, beat her, and cheat on her...
That's what it means to me...
I don't have that identity...
Who was supposed to teach that to me?
I had no Daddy's hugs, no Daddy's kisses,
and no Daddy's love...

Faithful and true!?
You must be kidding me.
Who was my example supposed to be?
Who was committed to me?
He said he was coming back...
Who was supposed to pick up the slack?
I had no Daddy's hugs, no Daddy's kisses,
and no Daddy's love...

A respectable member of society!?
Now please define that for me?
All I know is what I see on TV...
Crime, murder, hatred, and drugs are all
around me...

Now you tell me not to believe what I see?

You must be kidding me...

It's my environment that I see...

Who was supposed to provide for me?

I had no Daddy's hugs, no Daddy's kisses,

and no Daddy's love...

An example for me!?

How can this be?

Please explain that to me?

I had no Daddy's hugs, no Daddy's kisses,

and no Daddy's love...

You say there is one who knows how to love me?

How can He love a failure like me?

He loves me so much that He died for me?

You mean there is one who cares about me?

He'll give me Daddy's hugs, Daddy's kisses,

and Daddy's love...

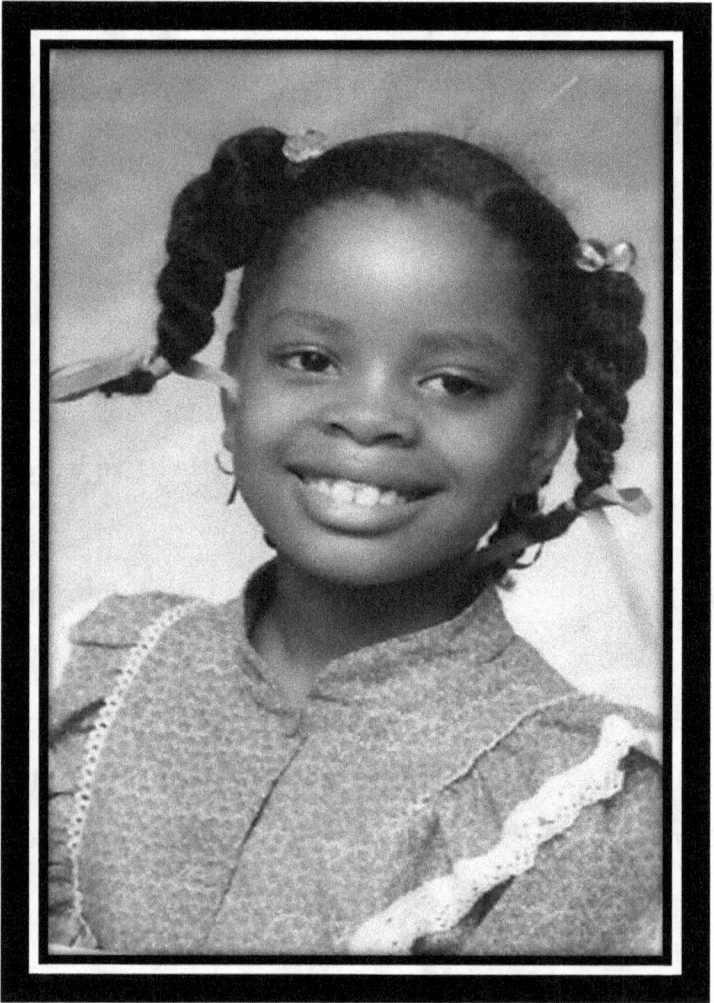

Earline Hall

Daddy's Hugs

*The Lord says, "I will guide you
along the best pathway for
your life. I will advise you
and watch over you."*
Psalm 32:8 NLT

Fathers are expected to provide love, nurturing, and caring for their children. The true father (Daddy) delights in his children. Fathers have a wonderful opportunity to teach, model, and mentor their children, displaying for them the heart and character of our heavenly Father. Throughout the Bible, we see fathers displaying great love and caring for their families, e.g. Abraham and Isaac (Genesis 22:1-19), or the father waiting for his prodigal son to return home (Luke 15).

It is from her father that the daughter gains her inner identity. She learns to relate to other men by watching how her father treats her mother. This is where she learns what to expect from a relationship with a male. If the father treats the mother with disrespect, the daughter learns to accept this treatment from men. On the other hand, if the father treats the mother with love and respect, his daughter learns to expect this treatment from men. What happens when the father fails to realize the importance of his role? What happens when he teaches his daughter to accept the wrong treatment from a man? What happens when he provides the wrong example for his son? Rather than building up their children, fathers often destroy their children. Sometimes they destroy the child's innocence and cause devastating harm. What happens that makes the person God has entrusted to protect you – violate you?

> *"But if in the field the man finds the girl who is engaged, and the man forces her and lies with her, then only the man who lies with her shall die. "But you shall do nothing to the girl; there is no sin in the girl worthy of death, for just as a man rises against his neighbor and murders him, so is this case. "When he found her in the field, the engaged girl cried out but there was no one to save her,"*
> Deut. 22:25-28 NASB

It is reported that a nine-year-old girl was raped and impregnated by her twenty-three-year-old stepfather with twins. She was given permission to abort the twins. Although abortion is illegal in the country where the girl lives, exceptions are made in cases where the mother's life is in danger or the fetus has no chance of survival.

Due to the structure of her young body, doctors were doubtful that she would have a full-term pregnancy. The doctor who confirmed her pregnancy said that it was a big risk for her to attempt to carry twins the full term. He also stated that the nine-year-old doesn't have the pelvis to support a gestation of twins.

According to police accounts, the girl's stepfather began abusing her when she was six-years-old. He paid her the equivalent of about fifty cents for each sexual encounter. The stepfather is currently in custody. What went wrong in this family?

The mothers bare the children, nurse them, and raise them primarily in their early years. She holds the household together by performing a wide variety of tasks. Yet, this does not negate the importance of the father during this period. Proverbs 31:10-31 gives us a good description of the honor due to the mother of the house. As she had to be quite aggressive to fulfill her role, she was far from docile and subservient. What happens to the children when a mother loses sight of her God-given role?

A man who was sought on charges that he repeatedly raped and molested his teenage daughter surrendered to police. The girl's mother was also arrested for allegedly aiding her husband in the sexual abuse. Both parents were charged with enticing a child for indecent purposes, rape, aggravated child molestation, sodomy, statutory rape, incest, and furnishing alcohol to a minor. They were both held without bond.

> *Judas came straight to Jesus.*
> *"Greetings, Teacher!" he*
> *exclaimed and gave*
> *Him the kiss.*
> Matthew 26:49 NLT

It is alleged that the mother did nothing to stop the sexual assaults on her daughter. When the girl refused to have sex with her father, the mother is reported to have urged the girl to comply with the abuse. The father is accused of punishing the girl to make her conform to his sexual demands. He reportedly used his parental authority to make the victim stand upright in the middle of the room until 3 o'clock in the morning. This technique was used to weaken the victim's resolve and encourage her to relent.

The parents are also accused of giving their daughter vodka. It was also reported that the mother moved out of the bedroom that she shared with her husband. This allowed the father to move the girl into the bedroom so he could continue his sexual assaults. What would cause a parent to violate a child in this way?

The steps of the godly are directed by the LORD. He delights in every detail of their lives.
Psalm 37:23 NLT

How will these children know what a good mother is supposed to be? Who showed them what a family was meant to be? Who defined their femininity? Who gave them what children need from their parents? There are many holes inside of these children that will need spiritual and emotional healing. There are hidden pains that no one may ever physically see. Who will help them developed a healthy identity? Who will help them understand what God intended motherhood to be? A good mother gives careful thought to the person that they choose to father their children. When parents fail, God still cares.

> *Father, teach us how to love those that you have placed in our care. Help us to be the parents that You have called us to be. Help to be a godly example to our children. Help us to bring our children up in fear and admonition of You. Give us the desire to reference and respect You. Father, help us not to provoke our children to wrath. Help us to correct them in love. Help us not to misuse or abuse the little ones that You have entrusted to our care. We acknowledge the need for Your intervention. Direct our path as we seek to raise Your children.*

Water

La'Toya Hall

I've seen it all; I've heard it all.

I know-it-all; I've touched it all.

I've traveled the globe; I've been all around.

I can be helpful; I can be hurtful.

I can keep you alive; I can make you die.

I always get used but I have never been
hurt.

I can be ice cold; I can stop you like snow.

I flow free like rain; now ask me my name.

Everyone knows me; I know everyone.

I fill the oceans; I am H2O.

Now that you know, it's time to go.

The cycle continues.

Admitted Molesters vs. All American Men

	Admitted Child Molesters	American Men
Married or formerly married	77%	73%
Some College	46%	49%
High School only	30%	32%
Working	69%	64%
Religious	93%	93%

Sources: The Abel and Harlow Child Molestation Prevention Study and the 1999 U.S. Census Statistical Abstract

Note: All people in both groups were at least 25 years old.

I've Heard it All

*When darkness overtakes the
godly, light will come bursting in.
They are generous,
compassionate, and righteous.*
Psalm 112:4

There is an old saying that says, "I've heard it
all!" We often feel that we have seen and heard it all.
My Aunt Bobbie proved on more than one occasion that
there is always room for the element of surprise. She
never failed to do or say something shocking. That is a
polite way of saying that she could easily embarrass
both family and friends by her actions. She holds the
record for saying the most shocking things that I have
ever heard. They are too shocking to repeat now.

*Death and life are in the power
of the tongue: and they that love
it shall eat the fruit thereof.*
Proverbs 18:21

Our words are a powerful tool. They can be an
instrument of harm or help. They can cause healing and
devastation. They can pronounce blessings and they can

pronounce curses. Words can build you up and they can tear you down. They can leave invisible scars that cause visible pain.

> *But ye shall receive power, after that the Holy Ghost is come upon you: and ye shall be witnesses unto me both in Jerusalem, and in all Judaea, and in Samaria, and unto the uttermost part of the earth.*
> Acts 1:8

God gave us the tool that is needed to bring correction in the lives of our children. I found the rod that I needed to bring about correction in Herman's life. The rod of correction was the little member in my mouth. My tongue began to speak life to him. My words began to speak blessings into his life. Rather than speaking threats, I began to call him on the telephone to speak

blessings over his life. At home, I constantly reminded him of who he is in Christ Jesus. This is how the rod (my tongue) brought about correction.

"Herman, do you know who you are?"

"Do you know that you are a fine young man?"

"Do you know that you are a handsome young man?"

"Do you know that you are going to make a wonderful father and husband?"

"Do you know that God is going to use you to travel the world and bring souls to Christ?"

"Do you know how many souls you are going to win for the Lord?"

"Do you know the anointing and call that God has placed upon your life?"

"Herman, do you know that you are going to be mightily used by God?"

"Do you know that you are the head and not the tail?"

"Do you know that you walk above and not beneath?"

"Do you know that you are the only Jesus some people will ever see?"

"Do you know that God has made choice of you?"

"Herman, do you know who you are?"

If he didn't know the answer to these questions, he found the answers. You would think that a child raised in the church almost from birth would have known who he is in Christ. He knows the Word. However, he needed to hear them spoken to him and reinforced in his life.

> *Simon Peter replied, "Lord, to whom would we go? You have the words that give eternal life."*
> John 6:68 NLT

For years, I had spoken other words into his life. I never had a shortage of words. The other messages that he had heard from me were quite different. My words were harsh and often cruel.

"You hard headed disobedient child!"

"You're the hardest head child that I have ever met!"

"Your head is harder than mine ever was!"

"You see what I am going through! You see how you treat me! Your children are going to treat you worse!"

"You are going to reap what you are sowing!"

"I'm never going to keep your children!"

"I'm only having one grandchild, and I already have that one."

He calmly responded, "I'm never going to have children."

Rather than helping Herman, my words were causing him pain. Out of desperation, I lashed out at him. My words were causing more harm. I never used profanity to address him. Yet, my words amounted to verbal abuse.

We pass many of our negative attitudes and behaviors on to our children. Herman didn't adopt all of my negative behavior. He has a very different role in the family. Herman is a real charmer. While he acts out the dysfunction in the family, he is also warm, sensitive, and affectionate. He is a very giving, loyal, and compassionate friend. He prefers to discuss only the positive that he sees in people. He doesn't like to discuss anything negative. Yet, he's a good listener and people share their problems with him. His words usually provide healing and encouragement.

A fool hath no delight in
understanding but that his heart
may discover itself.
Proverbs 18:2

One of the biggest challenges for parents is getting their children to listen. Every parent encounters a situation where no matter what they try to say or do, their child "refuses to listen". Many parents will just throw up their hands in frustration and say that they have a rebellious child who refuses to listen. Others will attempt to use strict forms of punishment as a way of communicating with their children. Still, others will try to bribe their children to behave. In the end, there is no "right way" to get your children to listen to you. Every child is different, and parents have to learn what works most effectively with their children. In dealing with Herman's behavior, I had to examine my past behavior. If a chosen method of discipline failed to correct my negative behavior, it was ineffective with him. If possible, he was more resistant to the discipline.

Several years ago, Earline's car broke down as my children were driving home from college. As Earline slept, Herman was driving at some accelerated speed. When she woke up, the car was slowing down until it finally stopped along the interstate. Herman informed his sister that he had almost won a race against another vehicle. We are not sure how fast the car was traveling. The speedometer flipped over at around 115 mph.

> *Thou wilt shew me the path of life: in Thy presence is fulness of joy, at Thy right hand there are pleasures for evermore.*
> Psalm 16:11

It was a Sunday afternoon when they called me. They were near Newnan, Georgia, south of Atlanta, and about 60 miles north of Columbus. For some reason, the telephone circuit to our roadside service was busy. I continued calling but I was on my way to bring them and the car home. By the time I reached them, I was still unsuccessful in reaching the roadside service. After being unable to repair the car on the spot, I gave Earline her instructions.

"Place the car in neutral and turn on the emergency flashers! I'm going to push the car to Columbus. It's getting dark and we're not going to be stuck here at night!"

See how very much the Father
loves us, for He calls us His
children, and that is what
we are!
1 John 3:1 NLT

Herman knew that he was at fault. The car overheated and he chose to ignore it. That coupled with his love for Earline made him climb in the back seat of the car. He didn't want her to ride alone. It never occurred to me that we wouldn't make it home safely. With Mama and La'Toya in my new Maxima, I pulled up behind her. I pushed the car down the interstate. I pushed the car to the shop in Columbus.

Along the way, there was only one glitch. As we turned from Airport Thruway onto Veterans Parkway in

Columbus, a police officer was stopped at the adjacent red light. Earline managed to hide the push by turning into a vacant parking lot. After the officer passed, we completed the trip without any further glitches.

In approximately an hour, we made it home safely. However, I had to purchase a new tag for the front of my car. There was no additional damage caused to either vehicle. **Warning, please don't try this stunt!** This was just one of those times that I responded out of necessity. God was with me in my foolishness. Earline had one thought all the way to Columbus.

"I'm going to die in front of my child!"

By the grace of God, we arrived in Columbus safely. I am trusting in that same grace to break every curse that has attached itself to my seed.

Not only must parents pray for the godly development of their children, they should praise and encourage them in the many small steps that they take in getting there. God has given us our tongues to use as a rod of correction. Death and life are in the power of the tongue. Our words can destroy and they can heal. The rod of correction did what God said it would do. When I began to speak life instead of death, my child found life. When I began to sow words of love and encouragement into his life, I began to reap the harvest. Sometimes, the progress seemed slow but I continued to speak life. On the hard days, I spoke more words of life.

At eighteen, Herman beautifully developed a relationship with God. He became a soul winner and a prayer warrior. He spent many nights asleep on his knees. He has a beautiful sweet spirit. He's no longer afraid to have children. One day, he will marry and have

his own family. I'll never excuse him for not being a *Real Man*. By the grace of God, he will never abuse his wife or walk away from his children. To the glory of God, those curses aren't lingering over his life. He has eight godchildren.

*When pride cometh, then cometh
shame: but with the lowly
is wisdom.*
Proverbs 11:2

Mama and Herman have always been good friends. They have deep conversations. Mama likes to ask for Herman's perspective and opinion. A few months ago, my mother had a conversation with Herman. She was telling him about the expectations and demands of adult children.

During the course of the conversation, she asked him, "When do your children grow-up? When do they stop expecting you to give them gifts?"

He responded very gently with sincerity in his voice, "Grandmamma, your children will always be your children, no matter how old they are."

Laughingly, Mama replied, "I forgot who I was talking to!"

> *But the lovingkindness of the LORD is from everlasting to everlasting on those who fear Him, And His righteousness to children's children,*
> Psalm 103:17

The devil has not relinquished his quest to destroy my child. In the midst of it all, I trust, lean, and depend on Jesus to break the curse that seeks to destroy him. To God belongs all the glory for what He has done in his life and all the things that He is going to do. I speak to every generational curse that seeks to destroy him and my future descendants:

> *You have no power, dominion or control over the inheritance that God has given me. The seed of my womb is blessed. The seed of my womb will bless God. The seed of my womb will live a righteous and*

sanctified life. My seed is a royal seed, a holy generation set apart for the work of the Lord. Every curse that has sought to bind, kill, and destroy them has been cursed from the very root. Because they are covered by the blood that Jesus shed on Calvary, no weapon that is formed against them shall prosper. All things are working together for their good. Everything negative that has been said to them, about them, concerning them and their future is canceled. The curse is broken!

78

Only by pride cometh contention:
but with the well advised is wisdom.
Proverbs 13:10

It Happened to me!

There was a secret that God gave me...
It was something special inside of me...
He placed a special beauty within me...
It wasn't for the whole world to see...
But then something happened to me...
It happened to me!

He put hidden treasure in me...
It was hidden deep inside of me...
It was hidden for only my husband to see...
One day he would discover me...
But something happened to me...
It happened to me!

He made and clothed me with innocence,
you see...
That was all He wanted me to be...
There were other things around me...
They were never meant to harm me...
Yet something happened to me...

It happened to me!

Before my husband ever found me...
Before I knew what I would be...
It came to destroy the love inside me...
It came hoping that I would never be free...
You see, something happened to me...
It happened to me!

There was a demon lurking nearby...
This demon my soul would try...
My beauty he didn't want to buy...
It was my treasure he wanted to try...
But then something happened to me...
It happened to me!

This demon made me cry...
I thought my very soul would die...
It even made me give depression a try...
It wanted me to hang my head and die...
Don't you see? Something happened to me!
It happened to me!

This demon wanted me to hide...

Shame was on his side...

Fear was held deep inside...

Forget! Well, I tried...

Don't you understand? Something happened

to me!

It happened to me!

For too long, silently I cried....

He stripped away all my pride...

All my innocence died...

He tampered with the treasure inside...

Something happened to me!

It happened to me!

One day, I could no longer hide...

For peace of mind, I cried...

Fear has got to subside...

Shame was where I could no longer reside...

Then something happened to me...

It happened to me!

With God on my side, I will no longer hide...

I'm taking back my pride...

This demon will no longer abide...

With His blood, I have been purified...

Something happened to me!

It happened to me!

Brothers and sisters don't you see...

You too can be free...

He's all that you need Him to be...

His grace is always free...

Let each victim say, something happened to

me...

It happened to me!

Let each victor sing with me...

The Son has made me free...

I'll be everything that God created me to

be...

He gave the victory to me...

Something happened to me!

It happened to me!

It Happened to me!

He lets me rest in green meadows,
He leads me beside peaceful streams.
He renews my strength.
He guides me along right paths,
bringing honor to His name.
Psalm 23:2-3 NLT

For too long, the subject of child molestation has been considered taboo. In Matthew 19:14, the Bible portrays children as the precious and innocent creations of God. Child molestation is the horrible monster that steals that innocence. In Leviticus 18, child molestation by a parent is condemned with the idea of incest. Child molestation committed by someone who is not related to you is condemned with adultery and fornication. Incest, having sexual relations with a family member, is condemned as harshly as any sin in the Bible. A person has to be sick mentally to take advantage of a child sexually. Child molestation is one of the most heinous sex crime ever committed. Truly, it is a crime against the innocent!

Each year, there are millions of children that are neglected or abused. These destructive and detrimental

84

experiences influence the innocent impressionable
child, increasing the risks for academic, behavioral,
emotional, physical, spiritual, and social problems
throughout their life.

*When thou saidst, Seek ye My
face; my heart said unto Thee,
Thy face, LORD, will I seek.*
Psalm 27:8

When Earline was a
baby, Ma'Dear would bathe
her in the kitchen sink. As
she began to talk, Earline
had one stipulation. No
males were allowed in
the house when she took
her bath. If she heard
what she perceived to be a
male voice, she screamed
as loud as she could.

Earline cried out,
"Don't come in this house!"

I don't know where she developed this phobia.
However, it may not have been such a bad idea. She has

never been sexually abused. It didn't matter if she recognized the voice. The fact is, very few molestations are done by strangers.

The perpetrator is usually a trusted adult or family member. This complicates and compounds the injury. Someone whom the child trusts has betrayed their confidence. The child's love and trust are violated, as well as their body. When the molester or rapist is a family member, the whole family is violated. The family is robbed and raped. The whole family will feel the pain and impact of the abuse. The victim may feel that they are suffering alone. This is not the case. The entire family suffers.

The molester may get the child to enter into a secret agreement or threaten to get the child into trouble if they reveal what has happened. The National Center on Child Abuse and Neglect defines child sexual assault as "Contacts or interactions between a child and an adult when the child is being used for sexual stimulation of the perpetrator or another person when the perpetrator or another person is in a position of power or control over the victim."

Do not have sexual intercourse

86

*with your sister or half sister,
whether she is your
father's daughter or your
mother's daughter, whether she
was brought up in the same
family or somewhere else.*
Leviticus 18:9 NLT

You may say, "Not in my family!" You may even be certain that there has never been a child molester or a molested child in your family. You may be sincere in that belief. You are probably sincerely wrong!

Unfortunately, most children will never tell. They feel ashamed and humiliated that this has happened to them. They are protecting their perpetrator because he or she is part of their family. They are also protecting other members of their family. They are saving them from the pain of knowing. In spite of the millions of victims in our families, many people stick to their mistaken belief that child molestation has nothing to do with them. I desperately wish that this were true.

An estimated one in twenty teenage boys and adult men sexually abuse children. It is estimated that one teenage girl or adult woman in every 3,300 females molests children. Although that's well over five million people, many families mistakenly believe that as far as molesters go, there has never been one in their family. They further believe that there never will be one. Add together the child victims, the adult survivors, and the perpetrators, and that's 15 out of every 100 Americans who have been either a molested child or a molester. That's a high probability that it will touch your family. To help break this curse and prevent child molestation from happening to the children closest to you, begin by telling others the basic facts.

> *Here on earth you will have many trials and sorrows. But take heart, because I have overcome the world.*
> John 16:33 NLT

Several years ago, I was facilitating a group of approximately twenty-five teenage girls. The group began discussing rape. In the course of the discussion, most of the girls present revealed that at least one person whom they trusted or who was trusted by their family had touched them in a way that would be considered inappropriate. The perpetrators were fathers, stepfathers, grandfathers, brothers, uncles, siblings' boyfriends, and the list went on. Where did these men learn this inappropriate behavior? On the other hand, more appropriately, why was it that they failed to learn appropriate behavior? Who was an example to them? Who was responsible for teaching them how to treat a young woman? Who was entrusted with the true responsibility of training them to be real men?

In the New Testament, Jesus refers to God as Abba, our equivalent to Dad, Papa, Father, or Daddy. This is an obvious term for a close and loving relationship. The paternal relationship was never meant to cause physical, emotional, social, or spiritual pain. God established the husband/father position as the provider for the family. The most important gift that the father provides to his children is love. Timothy teaches that a neglectful father was worse than a pagan was.

> *For all the law is fulfilled in one*
> *word, even in this; Thou shalt*
> *love thy neighbour as thyself.*
> Galatians 5:14

When I was teenage girl, vegetable-trucks brought fresh vegetables and fruit to the projects. They were a type of portable farmer's market. Usually, the truck stopped near the front door of our apartment.

Whenever the old man from across the ditch saw me at the truck, he was quick to purchase whatever I wanted from the vegetable man. Afterward he would invite me to come over to his house. I took the fruit but the look in his eyes warned me not to go that way. Ironically, his wife had taken us to church for many years. Her husband never went to church. This is just one example of the numerous times that men looked at me and I felt like a piece of meat.

I gave you your master's house and his wives and the kingdoms of Israel and Judah. And if that had not been enough, I would have given you much, much more. Why, then, have you despised the word of the LORD and done this horrible deed? For you have murdered Uriah the Hittite with the sword of the Ammonites and stolen his wife.
2 Samuel 12:8-9 NLT

Most sexual abuse is committed by people the child already knows such as friends, relatives, caregivers, teachers, clergy, trusted adults as well as complete strangers. The perpetrator may be an older child. There may also be more than one perpetrator within a family circle. When one perpetrator is known, it can be easy to overlook a new one.

Sexual abuse takes many forms and can involve forcing, coercing, bribing or threatening a child into sexual activity. The abuse often begins gradually and increases over time unless discovered. This may include someone being bold enough to say, "It happened to me!"

Physical evidence of sexual abuse is rare. It may include bladder and urinary infections, painful genitals, torn, stained or bloody undergarments. There is no one behavior that positively indicates a child has been sexually abused. Sudden or extreme changes in behavior should be considered as a possible reaction to abuse. Some children may not show any changes in behavior. They may never say, "It happened to me!"

Recently, I read an article about a man who was sentenced to consecutive life sentences for rape. He was fourteen-years-old when he was sentenced to twelve years in a facility for youthful offenders. He was charged with three counts of rape and four counts of burglary. As a child, he began raping. Twenty-four years later, the thirty-seven-year-old got three consecutive life sentences plus decades in prison after pleading guilty to similar crimes. During the years that elapsed between these sentences, he was convicted of numerous crimes. Was rape the prevailing pattern? It was!

But whoso shall offend one of these little ones which believe in me, it were better for him that a millstone were hanged about his neck, and that he were drowned in the depth of the sea.
Matthew 18:6

A child can be easily overlooked as a perpetrator, especially a family member. It's natural for children to play. They often play without direct adult supervision. The parents or guardians may be in a different room. The perpetrator may abuse with adults in the house. A child's abnormal obsession with one child can distract you from their true sickness. Yes, I am saying that the perpetrator is sick – mentally sick, sin-sick, morally sick, and socially sick. Obsessive telephone calls and unexplained or unexpected visits may be efforts to catch their victim in a vulnerable state.

When something just doesn't feel right, usually, it isn't right. Don't ignore your feelings or intuitions!

> *I say to myself, "The LORD is my inheritance; therefore, I will hope in Him!"*
> Lamentations 3:24 NLT

Don't jump to conclusions or make assumptions. Look for alternative theories or explanations. Ask questions of everybody in the house. Most of all listen to the answers. If the answers don't make sense or provide viable explanations, probe deeper. Don't give up! If after all of this, something still doesn't add up, ask the person with the suspicious behavior to stay away from your home. This may mean that you offend family or friends. It may also mean that you save a child from a molester. God is the only person in whom we can completely trust without reservation or doubt.

Tell Me
Earline Hall

Tell me why I was picked!
Was it because my skirt was too short,
or my hips too thick?

Tell me why it happened!
Was it because I am too friendly,
Or did my eyes seem to grab him?

Tell me what I did wrong!
I did nothing to have my life tossed around,
Like a ball in a game of Ping-Pong.

Tell me why you are talking about me!
Is it because it is too painful to accept,
It can happen to anybody.

Which Children Do Child Molesters Target?

CHILDREN IN THE FAMILY	
Biological Child	19%
Stepchild, Adopted or Foster Child	30%
Brothers & Sisters	12%
Nieces & Nephews	18%
Grandchild	5%
CHILDREN IN THE NEIGHBORHOOD	
Child Left in My Care	5%
Child of Friend or Neighbor	40%
CHILDREN WHO ARE STRANGERS	
Child Strangers	10%

Source: The Abel and Harlow Child Molestation Prevention Study

Who are These Molesters?

Better to be patient than powerful; better to have self-control than to conquer a city.
Proverbs 16:32 NLT

A national talk show host interviewed one convicted child molester. He confessed that he began preying upon boys he did not know when he was in his twenties. After he divorced from his wife, he molested his three-year-old daughter. He spent a number of years in jail for his crimes. During that time, he reports trying to reform himself. He told the host that he has not molested anyone in over twelve years. This may be true, given that he admitted that he has had the urge to molest. He further acknowledged that sex offenders are never cured.

For a good tree bringeth not forth corrupt fruit; neither doth a corrupt tree bring forth good fruit. For every tree is known by his own fruit. For of thorns men do not gather figs, nor of a bramble bush gather they grapes. A good man out of the

good treasure of his heart
bringeth forth that which is
good; and an evil man out of the
evil treasure of his heart
bringeth forth that which is evil:
for of the abundance of the heart
his mouth speaketh.
Luke 6:43-45

Several characteristics may signal the personality of a child predator. These may include but are not limited to the following:

> - Child predators are typically afraid of adult intimacy.
> - Child predators search out children who are vulnerable and easily manipulated.
> - A child predator may refuse to take responsibility for his actions.
> - Is most often an adult male.
> - Is usually married.
> - Works in a wide range of occupations, from unskilled laborer to corporate executive.
> - Relates better to children than adults.
> - Socializes with few adults unless they are pedophiles.
> - Usually prefers children in a specific age group.
> - Usually prefers either males or females but may be bi-sexual.
> - May seek employment or volunteer with programs involving children of the age of his preference.
> - Pursues children for sexual purposes.

- Frequently photographs or collects photographs of his victims, either dressed, nude, or in sexually explicit acts.
- Collects child erotica and child-adult pornography.
- May possess and furnish narcotics to his victims to lower their inhibitions.
- Is usually intelligent enough to recognize that he has a personal problem and understand the severity of it.
- May go to great lengths to conceal his illegal activity.
- Often rationalizes his illicit activities, emphasizing his positive impact upon the victim and repressing feelings about the harm that he has done.
- Often portrays the child as the aggressor. This usually occurs after the child realizes that by withholding "sexual favors", the child will obtain what he or she desires, such as new toys, clothing or trips.
- Talks about children in the same manner as one would talk about an adult lover or spouse.
- Often was a child molestation victim and frequently seeks out children at the age or stage of physical development at which he was molested.
- Often seeks out publications and organizations that support his sexual beliefs and practices.
- Usually corresponds with other pedophiles and exchanges child pornography and erotica as proof of involvement.
- Is usually non-violent and has few problems with the law (pedophiles are frequently respected community members).
- A child predator generally needs to control others.
- A child predator may have been abused as a child.
- A child predator often has a great desire for power.

➤ Child predators typically have low self-esteem.

Adults should be aware of the signs contained in the next section, which could indicate a child has been sexually molested. Some of these behaviors may have other explanations but it is important to assist the child no matter what the cause of these symptoms or behaviors.

➤ Acting out inappropriate sexual activity or showing an unusual interest in sexual matters
➤ Bruises, rashes, cuts, limping, multiple or poorly explained injuries
➤ Pain, itching, bleeding, fluid, or rawness in the private areas
➤ Changes in behavior, extreme mood swings, withdrawal, fearfulness, and excessive crying
➤ Fear of going to bed, or other sleep disturbances
➤ Seductive or "sexy" behavior towards adults or peers
➤ Withdrawal from family, friends, or usual activities
➤ Advanced sexual knowledge for the child's age
➤ Regressed behavior, such as bedwetting
➤ Eating disorders, eating very little or excessive eating
➤ Hostility or aggressive behaviors
➤ Drug or alcohol problems
➤ Suicidal thoughts or attempts
➤ A fear of certain places, people, or activities
➤ A sudden acting out of feelings or aggressive or rebellious behavior
➤ Regression to infantile behavior; clinging

➤ School or behavioral problems

Behavioral changes such as these may be due to causes other than child molestation such as a medical, family, social, or school problem. Children do not always demonstrate obvious signs such as these. They may do or say something that hints at the molestation. If a child suddenly becomes hysterical or violent towards another child or an adult, don't make assumptions. Ask questions. A perpetrator may make advances with others in the room.

When I was a teenager, this was often the case. Several of my friends were privileged to a peep exhibition. You may ask what a peep exhibition is. It is my way of saying that someone flashed their genitals to them. Hand manipulations often accompanied these shows. During many of these events, a family member of the flasher was present. He was always careful to hide this behavior from that relative. Because the flasher never touched them, they didn't consider this as abuse.

And He said, The things which are impossible with men are possible with God.
Luke 18:27

In my first book, *A Journey to Hell and Back*, I shared many of the painful details of my life. I touched briefly on being molested as a child. Yet, I did not elaborate on the details of the molestation. In spite of all of the intimate details of my life that were shared, there was a deeper secret that I was unable to share. It was a secret that many victims choose to hide. The shame and the pain of being raped were too hard to share. Like many rape victims, I internalized the pain. Rather than becoming angry with the attacker, I blamed myself. If only I wasn't in the wrong place... I should have known better... if only I hadn't gotten into the car... if only I hadn't had on that sexy outfit... I must have done something to lead him on... The list had no apparent end. Other things plagued my thoughts. Who will believe me? They will think it was my fault! Who can I tell? Who do I trust? Who will understand? In the end, I made the mistake of keeping silent.

Recently, a taxi driver was found guilty of drugging and sexually assaulting twelve female passengers. Investigators said the fifty-one-year-old man, may have attacked as many as five hundred women over his thirteen years as a cabbie. Why haven't his other victims come forward?

The following are reasons that other victims make this choice.

- ➢ They are too young to put what has happened into words
- ➢ They were threatened or bribed by the perpetrator to keep the abuse a secret
- ➢ They blame themselves or believe the abuse is punishment for being "bad"
- ➢ They feel too ashamed or embarrassed to tell
- ➢ They fear that they will be taken away from their family
- ➢ They are afraid no one will believe them
- ➢ The perpetrator promised gifts or rewards for keeping the secret
- ➢ They worry about getting into trouble or getting a loved one into trouble

Sometimes, we mistakenly assume that only women are rape victims. Recently, I was reminded of the error of this assumption. A gospel singer was on television. He was recounting his own pain – the pain of being molested as a child. Thirty years later, he's still receiving counseling.

In another recent news article, a couple who operates a babysitting service in their home was accused of taping themselves having sex with at least four children. The children ages ranged from two months to six years. The couple is being held on $100,000 bond.

Reported cases of child sexual abuse in the United States are estimated at 80,000 children each year, according to federal statistics. It is estimated that one in three girls will be sexually abused before she reaches the age of eighteen. An estimated one in six boys will be sexually abused before the age of eighteen. Regretfully, fewer than one in ten of these children will report the abuse. Sadly, most of these children will carry the emotional scars and guilt of abuse for the rest of their lives. Many of them (especially men) will sexually abuse others as adults.

During a recent public engagement, someone decided to disclose to me. After walking up to me, she began immediately to communicate her pain.

Undisturbed by the people passing by, she began, "You know, I could write a book about all the child molestation that I endured. When I was a little girl, my uncle started molesting me. It lasted until I was fifteen. He was in his forties. My daddy always called me his "good girl" because I did whatever any adult asked me to do. I never asked questions. Nobody talked about child abuse.

Years later, I saw my uncle at a family reunion. He was old and blind. I went over to speak to him. He reminded me of what he did to me as a child. He's dead now. My aunt is still living. She would be shocked if she knew what type of man that she married. When a family member abuses a child, it hurts the whole family. They blame the victim and support the abuser. It victimizes the child again. I've always been ashamed of what happened to me. It has only been recently that I have been able to share my story. I felt led to share this with you. It's time for someone to talk about it. It's time for the secrets to stop!"

After carefully listening to her story, I shared with her the nature of the book that I was writing. She asked me to share her story.

As she prepared to walk away, I asked, "Would you mind telling me how old you are?"

Smiling, she answered, "I'm seventy-five years old!"

The conversation had a profound and lasting effect on me. She looked much younger than the age that she provided to me. She was neatly groomed and well-manicured. Her outward appearance gave no indication of her inner pain. It was the first time that someone in this age group had disclosed to me such a deep pain – the pain of family secrets. It was a reminder of how deep the scars of abuse can be buried. It was a reminder that most abusers don't change. Even with his health hindering him from abusing another child, this perpetrator sought gratification in remembering his former conquests.

> *Love is patient and kind. Love is*
> *not jealous or boastful or proud*
> *or rude. It does not demand*
> *its own way.*
> 1 Corinthians 13:4-5a NLT

This story also gave me the reassurance and confirmation to move ahead with this project. It's time for the secrets to stop. It's time for the curse to be broken. It's time for families to stop protecting these molesters. It's time to protect and support our children. Encourage children to tell when they feel violated. Give them the benefit of being believed. Recently, I read that in 95% of the reported cases of child molestation, the report is true. There may be extenuating circumstances that will attribute to false reports. However, well-adjusted children seldom make false reports. Who would want to endure the pain, humiliation, and embarrassment that the victims are often forced to endure?

What can we do to keep our children safe? Remember, the person who abuses a child is to blame for the abuse, not the child! Always know the people who care for your children, including names, phone numbers, and addresses. We have to become actively involved and carefully supervise the child's activities. We have to be sensitive to changes in the child's behavior or attitude, paying close attention to our intuition indicating that something isn't quite right. Children have to be taught to listen to their intuition or "gut feeling" and communicate it to their parents. When a child says that they don't like someone, ask them to explain why and listen carefully. Teach children that it's okay to tell, no matter whom, no matter what! Talk about safety and sex with your child. Be sure to use proper names for genitals. Supervise and establish clear rules and guidelines for the child's computer use. Educate yourself (read, listen and ask) about child abuse.

Because of the courage, strength, and boldness of one young victim, I have been inspired to speak out. She has unknowingly encouraged me to face the demons of shame, guilt, blame, and defeat. Now, I can boldly say, "Something happened to me! It happened to me!" Today, I break that curse:

> *You filthy raping molesting spirit, you will not destroy my seed or offsprings. You have no place or authority in their lives. God has placed a hedge of protection around them and you no longer have access to them. You no longer have authority in their life. The Son has made them free. Shame, hurt, guilt, and embarrassment will not destroy them. Every curse that you bring with you is broken.*

It's Easier to Hide

It's easier to hide...
There's too much pain inside...
Some people call it pride...
The pain is eating me from inside...

Oh, that I might be free...
He keeps calling me...
My hidden pains, He can see...
Free! I would love to be...
Truth seems too hard for me...

It's easier to hide...
There's an emptiness inside...
In whom would I confide?
It's just easier to hide...
The hole keeps growing wide...

There is something that He wants from me...
Tell me what can it be?
What could He see in me?
Is it something that I can't see?
I can't trust me!

My failures surround me...

It's easier to hide...

My doubts won't subside...

It's not my pride...

It's just easier to hide...

Failure is where I reside...

Doesn't He Understand?

I see nothing in my hand...

Failure wasn't my plan...

Success isn't in this hand...

It's just easier to hide...

I never fail, if I haven't tried...

It's much easier to hide!

Easier to Hide

*And now, little children, abide in
Him, that, when He shall appear,
we may have confidence, and
not be ashamed before Him at
His coming.*
1 John 2:28

One day, someone very close to my heart was walking towards me. As they grew nearer, I felt so much pain, so much hidden pain. It can be easier to hide the pain that seeks to destroy us, sometimes we fear seeming weak or vulnerable. Rather than facing the pain and creating an opportunity or healing, we hide.

Because of the dynamics and complexity of puberty, teenage relationships, and other adolescent issues, a child molestation victim may be so distraught by the molestation that they will voluntarily disclose the abuse. Disclosure will often be to a school counselor, the non-offending parent, a pastor, to a trusted member of the family, a friend or, in some cases, it may even be to the authorities.

If a man happens to meet a

*virgin who is not pledged to be
married and rapes her and they
are discovered, he shall pay the
girl's father fifty shekels of silver.*
Deuteronomy 22:28-29

Whether the disclosure is voluntary or involuntary, there will be immediate reactions by the perpetrator. These reactions will range from denial to hostility. They may also attempt to protect their secret and obtain legal help. The most common line of defense for the perpetrator is, of course, denial. They can be very strong and convincing. In many cases, they are already gifted and habitual liars.

When there is an allegation of child molestation, there is a lot at stake. There are severe consequences to admitting the truth. It should be noted, the consequences are more severe if the truth is denied and later found to be true by the courts. In addition to the legal and social consequences, there is the possibility of publicity, financial difficulties, marital and family breakdown, loss of reputation, and civil charges. These give strong motivation for the perpetrator to lie.

The perpetrator may be a respected adult who will attempt to undermine the victim's account. In a

111

battle between an articulate adult and a child, in many ways, the child can often come out the loser. If the child is not believed, it compounds the injury.

A man is accused of molesting a relative and an eight-year-old boy who was a member of his Cub Scout den. He faces accusations that he committed indecent acts against seven additional children, all of whom he knew through Cub Scouts. At the time of his arrest, the man was forty-four years old. He was arrested on charges related to inappropriately touching and photographing the Cub Scout. It was also revealed that the man had allegedly molested another relative for an extended period.

He was charged with three counts of child molestation, four counts of aggravated child molestation and one count of sexual battery. Additionally, seven children came forward alleging acts ranging from being inappropriately photographed to acts of sodomy. These children range in age from six to nine years old. There are ten alleged victims. We applaud these young victims for daring to break the curse.

*Greater love hath no man than
this, that a man lay down*

his life for his friends.
John 15:13

Recently, I heard a story that warmed my heart. An eight-year-old child shared her pain with two friends. The two little girls were seven and eight years old. Even at this young age, they were true friends. They accompanied their friend to the guidance office of their school. Once there, they provided further support.

The first girl spoke bravely, "This is our friend and she has something that she needs to tell you!"

They requested permission to wait on their friend. As they watched their friend tearfully relate her story, one of the girls made another request.

Compassionately, she asked, "Can I just give her a hug?"

What an unselfish act of love. These young women acted with wisdom beyond their years. How many friends or family members have failed this test? How many people would have first considered their issues? How many people would have chosen to protect the molester rather than the child?

Another group would have taken this opportunity to show compassion to its opposite extreme.

Sadly, to say, recently I heard of another case at the opposite end of this spectrum. A young victim disclosed to an adult family member. The adult acknowledged that this sick behavior needed to stop and encouraged the victim to tell. Nevertheless, she did not provide the emotional or physical support to walk the victim through the process. Actually, she later became part of a conspiracy to discredit the victim. The perpetrator was her brother.

> *I sinned but it was not worth it.*
> *God rescued me from the*
> *grave, and now my life is*
> *filled with light.*
> Job 33:27 NLT

Families have a hard time accepting and believing that someone they know, love, and trust is a child molester or sexual predator. Many family members refuse to believe the child victims. They may blame them and do whatever it takes to protect the perpetrators. Most of the family members will eventually accept the reality. **CHILD SEXUAL ABUSE** affects the entire family system. The entire family requires empathy and education. Once the shock wears off, the recovery process can take years.

114

Depending on the severity of the denial, without the grace of God, some families will never recover.

> *But now I said to them, "You know very well what trouble we are in. Jerusalem lies in ruins, and its gates have been destroyed by fire. Let us rebuild the wall of Jerusalem and end this disgrace!"*
> Nehemiah 2:17 NLT

In order for the family to recover, the perpetrators must leave the family. This may only happen if criminal charges are filed. The perpetrators should only be allowed to return after they have had a great deal of therapy and held accountable before the courts. A board of professionals may need to approve their return to the family. Typically, perpetrators can only return if they take responsibility for their sexual abuse and have completed treatment successfully.

It is important to believe children when they say someone sexually abused them. It is important to under-react to the disclosure. If you react with outrage or shock, it may negatively affect the child. The seemingly nicest people you've ever known may be child molesters. ***Emotional availability*** is the key phrase for adults when children tell them about being sexually molested. Adults are helpful only when they respond to the children with empathy and compassion. The focus is the children. No matter how emotionally upset an adult may be, they must under-react. Afterward, adults can scream, cry, and do what they need to do to deal with their pain. However, in the presence of the children, their demeanor should remain one of alert concern.

How many people would have lied to protect the perpetrator? It is common for parents to lie to support their children. It is even common for siblings to lie to protect the perpetrator. This behavior often carries over from childhood into adulthood. Some parents will lie to protect their adult children. Rather than being bold or courageous enough to break the curse, they choose to help the curse remain intact.

Jim Mathews who mentored students at Clover County elementary schools faces charges of molesting a fourth-grade boy. Police arrested the sixty-three-year-old man on child molestation and aggravated sexual battery charges. The boy told police that his mentor brought him back to his home and molested him.

According to police, "There is no information that any criminal activity occurred on any school property or that they were aware of the molestation." School officials confirmed that the man had registered with the school system as a classroom mentor in 2007 and 2008. They also reported that the man has volunteered in two other school districts in the past. He was a foster parent, police said. In this county, school mentors help teachers organize activities, read with students and help tutor in math. Teachers supervise all volunteer activities.

"We did a background check on him and the background check was clear," one school official said. Police said, "Mathews had no prior criminal record. The boy has since transferred to another school district."

The man volunteered with the school system from 1998 until 2002. School records show Mathews passed a criminal background check in September 1998 and completed the school district's Adult Role Model for Students training. He also volunteered in Green and Spelling County Schools before July 2006, when the district started requiring background checks and keeping volunteer records.

No Harm... No Offense...

No harm meant to be given...
No offense should be taken...
If I knew better...
I'd do better...
This is just the way we do this thang...
Where I come from...

I was an addict before I was born...
I see nothing wrong with a lil' porn...
What's wrong with a life of crime?
I can do the time...
No harm meant to be given...
No offense should be taken...

You're related to me...
Sex with you should be free...
He's still blessing me...
He knows what they say about me...
If I knew better...

I'd do better...

My family supports my lies...
It's in sin that I thrive...
You owe me...
It's an entitlement, you see...
This is just the way we do this thang...
Where I come from...

I'll receive no harm...
I'll take no offense...
If you knew better...
You would do better...
This isn't the way we do it...
Where I come from...

Addict, you can be reborn...
You can be delivered from porn...
Change your criminal mind...
Before it's everlasting time...
Your harm has been given...
Offense has been taken...
I'm your cousin can't you see...

Sex with me should never be...

His blessings are always free...

It doesn't matter who you happen to be...

I'm telling you better...

Now do better...

Break free of your family's lies...

It's time that sin dies...

He knows how to pay...

If you continue to play...

This is the way He does it...

Where I come from!!!

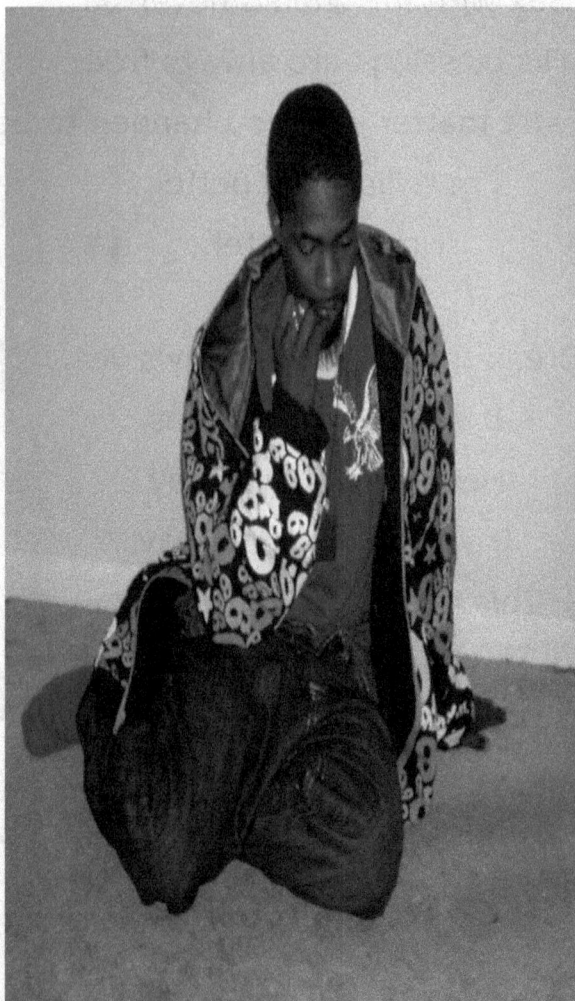

No harm meant to be given;

no offense should be taken...

No Harm... No Offense...

*Know ye not that the
unrighteous shall not inherit the
kingdom of God? Be not
deceived: neither fornicators, nor
idolaters, nor adulterers, nor
effeminate, nor abusers of
themselves with mankind, Nor
thieves, nor covetous, nor
drunkards, nor revilers, nor
extortioners, shall inherit the
kingdom of God.*
1 Corinthians 6:9-10

What's in a family? There are liars in a family. There are perpetrators of crime in a family. There are rapists in a family. There are backbiters in a family. There are adulterers in a family. There are whoremongers in a family. There are thieves in a family. There are blasphemers in a family. There are child molesters in a family. While this may not be in the nuclear family, it will be in the extended family. Every dysfunctional family has the potential to have a murderer, a rapist, and a child molester. There is envy, pride, jealousy, malice, and prejudice in a family.

122

Prayerfully, by the grace of God, there will also be love in a family.

If a child is molested within the family or by a stranger, it is likely that the child will feel the same sense of helplessness in both cases. They may believe that have no one to confide in. It is unlikely that a child who is being molested by a family member will immediately go to a parent. The dysfunctional family is not going to be open to listening because the family itself is keeping secrets. The child senses on some level that this will disrupt the family system of denial within the family. If a family member is a molester and one of the parents does something about it, the child and the family member are not the only ones affected by the abuse. The entire family system is affected.

Some scientists believe that people think and behave in certain ways because they are taught to do so. This is known as the "nurture"

theory of human behavior. They are taught to behave certain ways. Other scientists think that people behave as they do according to genetic predispositions or even "animal instincts." This is known as the "nature" of human behavior theory. My own version of these theories is "where I come from" theory. The notion of nature, therefore, refers to the biologically prescribed tendencies and capabilities that each individual possesses, which may unfold throughout the course of their life. They believe that we inherit certain behaviors.

Nurture refers to various environmental or external factors to which an individual is exposed from conception to death. These environmental factors involve multiple dimensions. They include both physical environments (e.g., drug usage and prenatal nutrition) and social environments (e.g., schools and friends). To complicate matters further, the factors in each of these areas are influenced by other elements. The kind of peers a child is exposed to may depend on their parents' view of what ideal playmates should be.

You will keep in perfect peace all
who trust in You, whose
thoughts are fixed on You!
Isaiah 26:3 NLT

Through our families, we learn the basics of developing relationships. However, we sometimes develop strategies to help us cope with difficult or "dysfunctional" family situations such as parents who are critical, abusive, manipulative, neglectful, controlling, drug addicts or alcoholics.

When Bryce also known as B-Hugs, was accused of being a child molester and rapist, it shook our family to the core. When I first learned of the accusations, I thought I had heard another name. As I tried to awaken myself from my sleep, I wanted to go back to sleep. I wanted to pretend that I had misunderstood the disclosure. It had to be a bad nightmare. Surely, no one so close to me would deliberately violate their family's trust. So many people would be hurt. So many people would be shocked. The ramifications were more than I could fathom so early in the morning. It would be better if I went back to sleep. That wasn't an option. It would be months before my sleep would return to a normal pattern.

For years, I have stood up for the underdog. I have been outspoken on AIDS, domestic violence, child abuse and neglect, rape, and so many social issues.

What was I to do now? Was I to disregard all of the well-meaning advice that I had given to others? Should I allow my love for the perpetrator to color my response? How would I ever be able to help another victim if I ignored this one?

My attention was turned immediately away from Bryce. Instead, my thoughts began to focus on his mother. This would hurt her deeply. How could I lessen her pain? There were other siblings to consider. What about their hurt and pain? Had any of them been abused? Were they still in danger? My love for them tore at my heart. Could I ignore what I had been told?

A child had been violated. A child's innocence had been destroyed. Ignoring what he had done would cause additional harm to the child. A criminal complaint or investigation could also be devastating to the child. An entire family system would be forced to choose sides. The family was in danger of permanent destruction. These issues had already caused the child to keep the secret. Now, the secret was out. It wasn't a dream. It was a nightmare. However, it wasn't night. Actually, what had been hidden in darkness had come to the light. It had to be addressed. It wasn't going away.

*With my soul have I desired
Thee in the night; yea, with my
spirit within me will I seek Thee
early: for when Thy judgments
are in the earth, the inhabitants
of the world will learn
righteousness.*
Isaiah 26:9

A father told police in April 2008 that he kept his daughter prisoner in a cellar apartment for twenty-four years. He fathered seven children with her. He was charged with murder in the death of one child who died shortly after birth. He faced other charges regarding his daughter's captivity and abuse. Three of the surviving children were imprisoned with his daughter in a cell beneath the home. The other three children were raised by the man and his wife. He reportedly told his wife the children had been abandoned.

*Therefore I say unto you, What
things soever ye desire, when ye
pray, believe that ye receive
them, and ye shall have them.*
Mark 11:24

Dysfunctional families cause lots of harm. They cause lots of hurt. They cause many offenses. What do you do when a person who meant no harm causes you harm? What do you do when a person who meant no offense causes you offense? Receive no harm. Take no offense. Stand on the Word of God and receive the salvation of God. Pray for the person who has caused you harm. Pray for the person who has caused you offense. Pray twice as hard for the person who taught them how to cause offense or harm.

The devastation caused to my family was worse than anything I could have imagined. Denial was expected. The pain was expected. Hurt was expected. However, I never expected innocent people to suffer. In my ignorance, I expected a speedy resolve to the case. When something of this magnitude happens, there are a number of things that can hinder or influence the investigation and prosecution of the case.

Early in the case, the behavior of the investigators who respond to an allegation of sexual abuse is pivotal in terms of how the case progresses and is ultimately resolved. Things within the investigator's background may influence the investigation. A faulty investigation may result in innocent children being damaged and innocent people being falsely charged and guilty people being acquitted. A good investigation is likely to result in an accurate resolution of the case.

Some things within our environment and our heredity will hinder justice. The influence of our environment can be a curse. It has the potential to keep us trapped in negativity. It can be hard to accept the need for a different type of friend or neighborhood. I break this curse from my family.

> *To every curse of heredity and environment, I break your attachment. Environmental influences will not destroy my seed. Hereditary influences will not destroy my seed. We have been healed from every hurt and offense in our environment. We will not cause harm or offense because of where we come from. Every unsavory influence that has sought to hinder my seed and me no longer has any influence over our lives. We will prosper and excel at everything God has given us to do. Your curse has been broken.*

Secrets, Secrets
Lyrical Payne

I've got secrets, secrets.

Secrets so deep my blood can't find 'em

I've got secrets, secrets.

Secrets so private my breath can't breathe

'em

I've got secrets, secrets.

Secrets so bad my tongue don't dare speak

'em

I've got secrets, secrets.

Secrets so dark my eyes wish they'd never

seen them

I've got secrets, secrets.

Secrets so painful it hurts to touch them

I've got secrets, secrets.

Secrets so horrible my ears bleed to hear

'em

I've got secrets, secrets.

Secrets so precious the bank can't hold 'em

I've got secrets, secrets.

Secrets so scandalous paparazzi won't use

'em

I've got secrets, secrets.

Secrets so erasable my pencil can't write

'em

I've got secrets, secrets.

Secrets so unclear I'm unable to outline 'em

I've got secrets, secrets.

Secrets so expensive my bags can't carry

'em

I've got secrets, secrets.

Secrets so dirty they can't be bleached out

I've got secrets, secrets.

Secrets so indefinable the dictionary has no

words for 'em

I've got secrets, secrets.

Secrets so life changing I have to let them

out!

Secret Secrets

Others trusted God and were
tortured, preferring to die rather
than turn from God and be free.
They placed their hope in the
resurrection to a better life.
Hebrews 11:35 NLT

Dysfunctional families have many secrets. They will go to extreme lengths to keep the family secrets. The fear of their secrets being exposed may be the greatest motivating factor for their behavior. Every family has some secrets or things that they consider private family business. Dysfunctional families have generational secrets that are maintained.

There was a woman that I knew. To simplify the story, we will call her Miss Martha. She had at least seven children. The children may have had as many as six different fathers. We will never know. She had secrets.

Miss Martha never married. She was raised in a home with her mother and father, Sarah and Larry Grant. At various times, other family members also lived in the home. After Larry's death, Martha and

Sarah continued to live together. Sarah, Martha's mother was blessed with long life.

Martha's older children report that their youngest sibling was born at home. They never knew that their mother was pregnant. According to their memories, one day, they heard the sound of crying coming from the bedroom. The sound reminded them of a cat. It was at that point, they learned about the new addition to the family.

A gentle answer deflects anger
but harsh words make
tempers flare.
Proverbs 15:1 NLT

As the children grew older, they began to ask questions about their fathers. One of Martha's children was raised by his father's family. This later became a source of pain to that child. He never understood why Martha had given him away and kept the others. Sarah provided the two youngest children with the name of their father. Their father's name was Danny. He lived nearby in Phenix City, Alabama. The other children lacked this information. As the children grew older and began to have children and grandchildren, the secrets remained. There were rumors about the various fathers. It was rumored that some children shared the same father. Physical features and characteristics offered very little indication. Martha seemed to ignore their questions. She would remain quiet whenever the children's fathers were mentioned. Her facial expressions remained unchanged. She never seemed tempted to provide answers. With each new generation, Martha's grandchildren had questions. Martha was unmoved and held on to her secrets.

The grandchildren were often curious and determined to find answers. On more than one occasion, one of them was sure that they had discovered their grandfather's name. Martha's youngest child, Linda was a great comedian. If she had been born during a different time perhaps this would have been her vocation. When one of Linda's nieces, Hannah, began to question Martha about her grandfather's name, Linda decided to have some fun with her. She told Hannah that she would introduce her to her grandfather. Linda asked Hannah to drive her to Danny's house. Hannah was so excited about meeting her grandfather. Hannah ran to hug her (fake), grandfather. Danny didn't know what was going on but he didn't say anything. When Hannah shared her good news with the other grandchildren, they wondered if it was possible, Danny was their grandfather, too.

Martha was sitting in her favorite chair in the living room. Behind her was the glass door that led to

the balcony. As Hannah relayed her happiness, Martha sat quietly. As other grand- children began to look for some glimmer of hope that the secret had finally been revealed, Martha kept quiet. Martha's other children knew that Linda had lied to Hannah.

Not only was Hannah devastated when she learned the truth, the other children were equally disappointed.

*"Why don't you talk to me?"
Pilate demanded. "Don't you
realize that I have the power to
release you or crucify you?" Then
Jesus said, "You would have no
power over Me at all unless it*

were given to you from above."
John 19:10-11 NLT

Years later, another granddaughter thought she had discovered the truth. She had taken her grandmother to apply for social security benefits. In the absence of other supporting documentation, school records were needed. When the granddaughter noticed the father's name listed on the school records, she was so excited. She finally knew her grandfather's name. She couldn't wait to tell Martha that she had discovered her secret. Her grandmother only smiled as her granddaughter went to confront Martha with this information. Again, Martha just sat there in her chair. She gave no indication that she heard one word that was said. In the young woman's excitement, she had failed to notice the mother's name listed on the record. Martha's name wasn't listed. The parents were listed as, Sarah and Larry Grant, Martha's parents.

It might seem that Miss Martha was a very promiscuous woman but the other things about her character suggest this was not the case. She worked hard to provide for her children. Miss Martha worked as a domestic aide, nanny, and cook for several prominent families in the community. She maintained a close relationship with these families throughout her life. She often earned extra money by ironing in her home. She kept her children and her house clean. She was a religious woman and active supporter of her church. She was not a consumer of strong drink or alcoholic beverages. She didn't smoke or dip snuff. She was never reported to be a woman who frequented nightclubs or bars. Her children didn't meet new uncles (boyfriends) on a regular basis. The older children had no indication of who fathered the younger siblings.

Martha never married or expressed regrets. She wasn't a bitter woman. She wasn't known for being a big gossiper. She was never accused of verbally or physically abusing her children. Actually, Martha's mother was the disciplinarian for the children. Martha never used harsh or profane words. This is not to imply that her children found no fault in her.

Martha was often accused of showing extreme favoritism among her children. It seemed that she was almost indifferent to some of her children. While Martha was not abusive to her children, her treatment of some of them bred on emotional neglect. These same feelings reflected in the way she treated her grandchildren. The favoritism was so obvious that the children she favored often resented her apparent lack of emotions toward the other siblings. Martha's mother was known by her children and grandchildren, as Mama. It was Mama's role to provide the love and nurturing that the children needed.

During her later years, one of Martha's elderly neighbors accused her of lying. She was so upset that she called the police.

When the officer arrived, he asked, "Can you tell me exactly what she said to you?"

Struggling for words, Miss Martha replied, "She called me something that means I was telling a story!"

Again, the officer sought clarification, "What exactly did she say?"

Miss Martha attempted to explain. She wanted the woman punished but could not allow herself to say the word. As he drove away, the police officer must have been laughing. Standing nearby watching the incident, I was doing exactly that, laughing.

I have cared for you since you were born. Yes, I carried you

before you were born. I will be
your God throughout your
lifetime—until your hair is white
with age. I made you, and I will
care for you. I will carry you
along and save you.
Isaiah 46:3b-4 NLT

Although Martha lived to be almost ninety-years-old, she never discussed her secrets. She took the secrets to her grave. There were many rumors, the mailman, the son of people that she worked for, the milkman, etc. Her descendants will never know the truth. Those who may have had some clues chose to keep the secrets. They too have now passed on. Miss Martha had many relatives that lived in the home with her during that time. For some reason, they didn't know the answers or chose not to share them. Future generations will ask the same questions that have been asked before but no answers will come. The answers were buried a long time ago. They were buried years before Miss Martha was buried at Green Acres Cemetery in Columbus, Georgia. They were buried in her heart.

As I'm writing this book, I wonder if there was a reason that Martha protected her secrets. I ask myself if

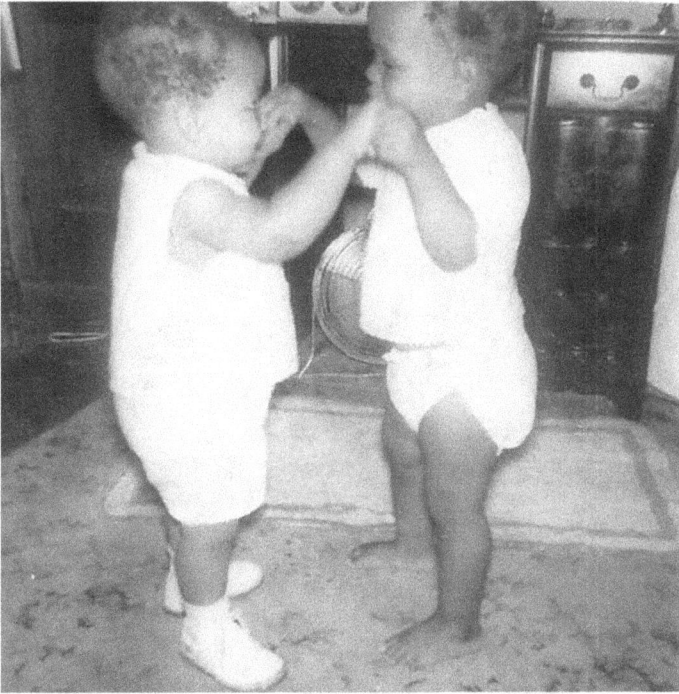

the way that she treated her children was a reflection of her feelings for their fathers. She was born during a time when some subjects were taboo. Some things were kept hidden. They were kept secret. Perhaps her secrets were too painful to share. Martha's story may be a common story. If she were alive today, I wonder if she would say, "It happened to me! It happened to me!"

Lil' Earline

Tattletale

Lyrical Payne

My name is tattletale

They say I tattletale

I tell all the details

My name is tattletale

If it's juicy my memory, never fails

Cuz you know what they call me

My name is tattletale

If you want it secret, when you step on the

scale

Don't do it round me cuz I'm the tattletale

I'll tell all your secrets just like it's a

fairytale

Cuz you know what I am, man I'm the

tattletale

I'll read all your notes just like checking the

mail

I'm just sneaky like that, cuz I'm the

tattletale

If it'll get you in trouble, I'll put it up for sale

My name is tattletale,

Keeping secrets for profit, they call that
blackmail

But you know what they call me; my name
is tattletale

But you won't get any friends, whether male
or female

If you live your life being a tattletale

With all those secrets you'll probably burn in
hell

And so I changed my life don't call me
tattletale

But hey, it's not always bad to be a
tattletale

And if you think that it is, that myth I'm
gonna dispel

Cuz see I had my own secret I was afraid to
tell

And see now that I've told it, that man is
going to jail

But keeping this world safe don't make me a
tattletale

Tattletale

*And the people believed: and
when they heard that the LORD
had visited the children of Israel,
and that he had looked upon
their affliction, then they bowed
their heads and worshipped.*
Exodus 4:31

For far too long, too many people have ascribed to the notion that – children should be seen and not heard. Where this fallacy developed, I do not know. It is my intention to shatter that curse at its very core. Recently, I saw an enlightening bumper sticker. It read, "Children Should Be Seen, Heard...and Believed." That statement deserves exploration.

Tattle-telling is often viewed in a negative light. A tattletale is someone who tells tales. They may be true tales. They may be partially true tales. Tattling or "telling on" is commonplace for many five to ten-year-olds. They may not be telling the truth. Tattling is telling secrets. For many parents, it can be annoying. As children, we were taught that we shouldn't tattle on others. It only makes sense that we would continue to enforce this belief with our offsprings.

When my granddaughter was a baby, Herman often pushed her through the neighborhood in her stroller. As she grew older, he would still take La'Toya with him. It didn't matter that she was a *tattletale*.

Excitedly, she relayed this story, "I was walking down the street with Herman and Skeet. They decided to throw water balloons at a man's car. The man got mad. He started cursing and we had to run. I had to hide in the bushes with them until the man stopped looking for us."

This didn't stop Herman from taking her with him and it didn't stop La'Toya from being a *tattletale*.

He set my feet on solid ground
and steadied me as I
walked along.
Psalm 40:2 NLT

One night, we heard La'Toya crying in the den. When we investigated, there was blood streaming from a cut above her eye. She related this story.

Tearfully, she said, "It was Herman's fault. He was playing that loud dancing music. It made me feel like dancing. While I was dancing, I fell and hit my head on the table. It's Herman's fault. He knew that music would make me dance."

It was a glass coffee table. La'Toya wasn't seriously hurt. The next day, she received several stitches to close the wound. La'Toya loves Herman. During the early years of her life, she managed to relate everything back to Herman. The same person that was always telling on him was also his biggest supporter.

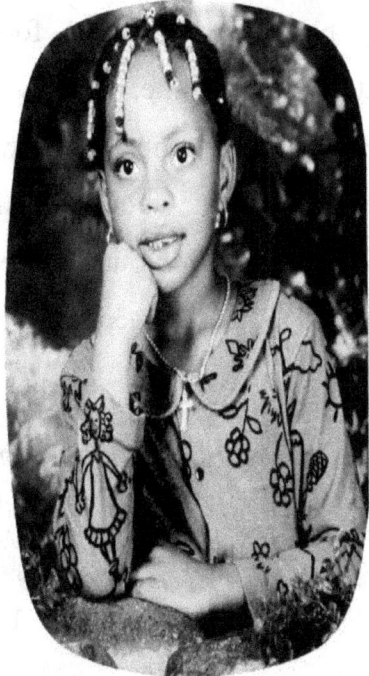

One day, we were riding down the street. I was giving Herman one of my lectures. He had grown accustomed to these. His normal response was, "Yes Mama." La'Toya had a different response.

In a very firm tone, she said, "You don't have to yell at my uncle!"

In September 2008, Polish authorities launched an investigation into a twenty-one-year-old woman's allegations that her father kept her prisoner for six years. She also reported that during her imprisonment, he repeatedly raped her. She said that she had two sons by her father but was forced to give them up for adoption. To some, she may be considered a *tattletale*.

Tattle telling is not wrong when there is a need to tell someone about something wrong that was done. We need to teach our children to tell things that have to be told to keep someone from getting hurt.

> *I will lift up mine eyes unto the hills, from whence cometh my help. My help cometh from the LORD, which made heaven and earth.*
> Psalm 121:1-2

A man was charged with incest and murder after authorities said he fathered four children with his teenage daughter. He was also accused of killing at least one of the babies. The investigation began when the girl's sister informed police of the alleged abuse. The teenager said that she waited until she turned eighteen years old to come forward because she was afraid of being placed in state custody.

The eighteen-year-old said her sister, now nineteen, was thirteen when their father started molesting her. The eighteen-year-old said her sibling confided in her about the abuse after becoming pregnant the first time.

The new owners of the property, where the family used to live, found the bodies of two infants. They were found in sealed coolers. One of the infants died after not receiving medical treatment for pneumonia.

The father has been charged with second-degree murder in the death of the baby that died from pneumonia. The forty-seven-year-old is also accused of fathering the other infant whose body was found. The cause of death has not been determined for that baby's death. Authorities believe a third baby was buried in a city where the family once lived. The fourth child is a three-year-old boy. He was placed in state custody.

In addition to the murder charge, the father also was charged with endangering the welfare of a child, statutory rape, and two counts each of incest and abandoning a corpse. He was being held in jail under a $500,000 bond. Charges were also brought against the forty-seven-year-old mother. She has been charged with endangering the welfare of a child. Authorities believe that she did little to stop her daughter's sexual molestation. She was freed on bond.

The eighteen-year-old sister was willing to take the risk. Because the sister risked being labeled a *tattletale*, this horrific crime was discovered.

> *But now, O Jacob, listen to the LORD who created you. O Israel, the one who formed you says, "Do not be afraid, for I have ransomed you. I have called you by name; you are mine."*
> Isaiah 43:1 NLT

Nobody wants to be disliked. Everyone likes to be accepted. However, it's not popular to be the kid that tells or snitches. Nevertheless, sometimes, it's the right thing to do. Imagine knowing something is wrong and not knowing whether you should tell someone. This is a problem children face every day. So when is it ok to tell? If children are encouraged not to tell, we risk losing valuable information. With that in mind, I say, "tell, tell, tell..." Children should tell and tell until somebody listens.

> *If you need wisdom . . . ask Him,*
> *and He will gladly tell you.*
> James 1:5 NLT

We have all heard the story of "the boy who cried wolf." He cried out for help one time too many. When the real threat came, it was hard to believe him. Certainly, children should understand the consequences of lying. However, when children make alarming or shocking disclosures, they should be believed. We have heard of the legal system that a person is innocent until proven guilty. When a child discloses a devastating secret, the opposite position should be assumed. It should be assumed that the child is telling the truth unless it can be proven beyond a reasonable doubt that the child lied.

A forty-five-year-old father was detained after his wife and daughter made a police report. The mother told a television station that she learned what was happening when she found her daughter's diary. She also reported that her husband physically assaulted her when she confronted him. The mother said that the father intimidated them. He was also accused of making death threats against the daughter. These threats were to keep her from disclosing the abuse.

Seek His will in all you do, and
He will direct your paths.
Proverbs 3:6 NLT

When parents or adults minimize the abuse, it allows the cycle of abuse to continue. There are many reasons why children don't tell. Perpetrators may tell children lies to scare them into silence. Sometimes they may threaten to harm the child's family if the abuse is revealed. Some children think if they tell about child sexual abuse -the abuse will get worse. They fear that the perpetrators will carry out their threats. Others fear their parents will not love them anymore. The child may fear they will be yelled at or they will be blamed. The abuser may be successful in convincing the child that their parents will not love them anymore. They may be concerned that their parents will be upset and they don't want to upset their parents. They may even fear that their parents might die of the shock

> *His own iniquities shall take the*
> *wicked himself, and he shall be*
> *holden with the cords of his sins.*
> *He shall die without instruction;*
> *and in the greatness of his folly*
> *he shall go astray.*
> Proverbs 5:22-23

Let me relate another sad story. The events at the Cinnamon County courthouse told the story of a family and community ripped apart by child molestation. The defendant, seventy-four-year-old Calvin Hill, of Wellborn, maintained his innocence, even as he was being sentenced to what may be a life sentence for him. He was sentenced to serve twenty-five- years in prison.

"I can't say I'm sorry! I didn't do it," asserted Hill.

He was convicted of molesting his granddaughter from the age seven to nine, and a grandson, from age three to five. This abuse has caused a rift in the family. His son and daughter-in-law are now estranged from most of their extended family. This often occurs when a family member sexually abuses a child. Family members take sides. The couple pleaded for justice for their children.

"I just ask that, for the crimes he's committed, he receive the maximum sentence," said his son Bradley Hill. Bradley is the father of the two victims.

"He has no idea what he's done to those kids," said Janet Hill, Bradley's wife. "He's destroyed us!"

District Attorney Heather Banner, who prosecuted the case, asked that the victims and community be protected and that a message is sent to all child molesters.

"He needs to be punished swiftly, severely and justly," she said.

The victims' parents have talked openly about the case. I hope that their openness will raise public awareness about the devastations of child molestation.

Defense attorney Robyn Littlejohn asked the judge to consider the minimum sentence possible, 10 years in prison.

She stated, "I think any sentence that the court imposes is going to be a life sentence for him."

Hill, a former cabinet refinisher, was convicted of fifteen felony counts for molesting his grandchildren.

He faced a potential two-hundred-year sentence. Superior Court Judge Harry Jacobs, who presided over the trial, followed the prosecution's recommendation of twenty-five years to serve in prison.

"It's unlikely the holes that you have ripped into your good and decent family will be mended for some time, if ever," Judge Jacobs told him.

> *Jesus Christ was delivered for*
> *our offenses, and was raised*
> *again for our justification.*
> Romans 4:25

It deeply saddens me to say that this story is all too common. Families often side with the molester. Denial may seem easier than accepting the truth. Families strive towards stability or a sense of normalcy. Denial may seem easier than dealing with other emotions – guilt, shame, embarrassment, and vulnerability.

Earline

Assumption Junction
Earline Hall

Don't tell me the family has secrets.

We don't have more than most.

In this family, we don't air dirty laundry!

To be a member you stand stoic at your

post.

It hurts to think of the word incest.

What happened was not really that bad.

It is not helpful to dwell on your past.

If you hold on to your grudges, you'll go

mad.

I am grateful you won't shame the family.

We are not the ones to blame.

I don't want to be involved with your

problems.

You don't need counselors or therapy.

It is just a money game.

Please do not use the word advances

Maybe they're just trying to be close

Don't tell me about family dysfunctions

We are the ones that love you the most

I am thankful the police aren't involved.

This is more of a family thing.

We will all stay away from the beast.

Maybe next time, another family will feel his

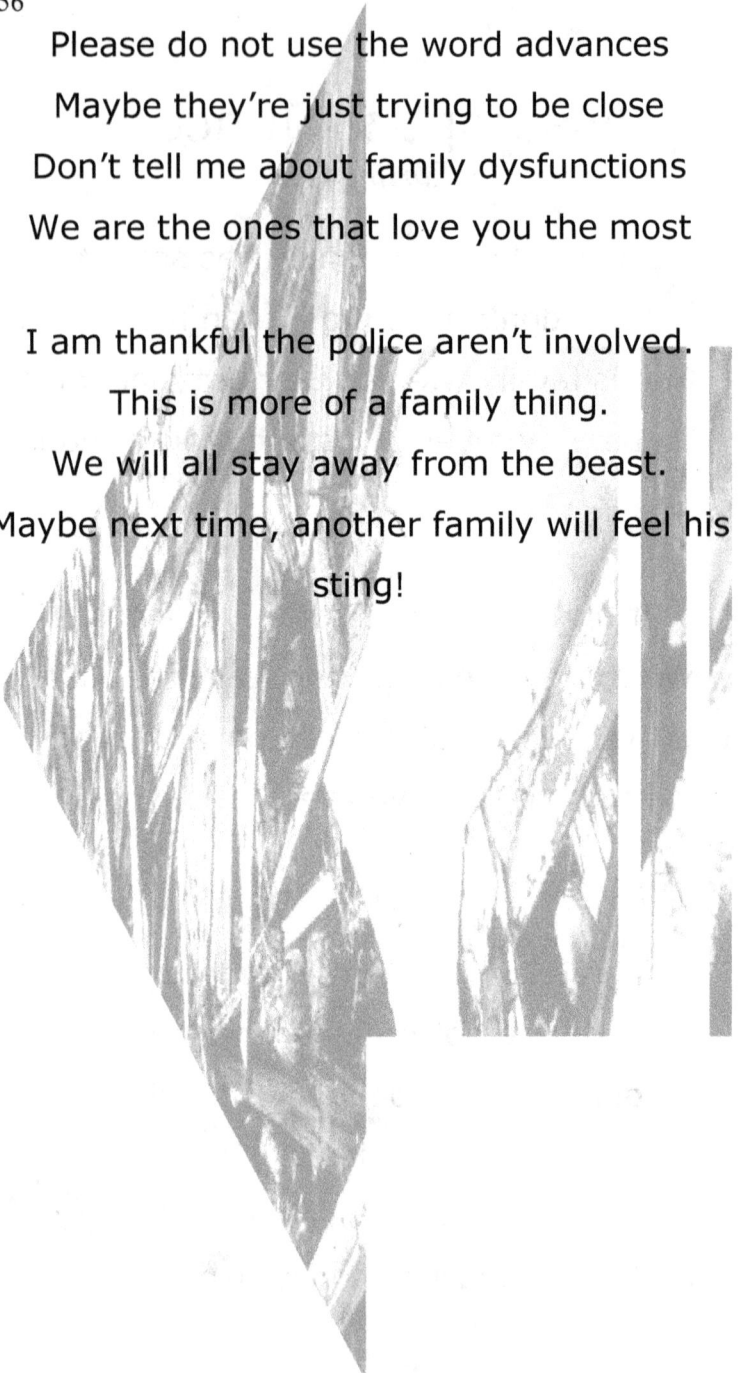

sting!

Assumption Junction

I am disgusted with my life. Let me complain freely. I will speak in the bitterness of my soul.
Job 10:1 NLT

Never assume that someone is telling the truth. Never assume that they are lying. Give everyone the benefit of the doubt. Give everyone the benefit of a second chance. As you do all of the things before mentioned, keep a straight face.

When Herman was in school, it became almost a routine pattern for me to receive complaints about his behavior. All my efforts to correct his disciplinary problems seemed useless. My frustration bordered on hopelessness. Rather than asking questions, I listened as they reported his new antics.

One day, I received a call from Herman's school.

The principle called with another negative report.

With exasperation in her voice, she said, "Herman is in trouble again! Today, he almost put another child's eye out. He hit the child with a stick. He's being suspended!"

With very few questions, I accepted what she said. Herman offered no explanation. He made no excuses.

> *See that none render evil for evil*
> *unto any man; but ever follow*
> *that which is good,*
> *both among yourselves,*
> *and to all men.*
> 1 Thessalonians 5:15

When Herman returned to school, he would often stay late after school. He was helping a teacher straighten up her classroom. One day, I had the opportunity to meet the teacher. She asked me a question that I have never forgotten.

Looking directly into my eyes, she said, "When Herman was suspended from school, why didn't you ask questions? The other child wasn't suspended. It wasn't an accident. The other child deliberately hit Herman with a stick between his eyes. Herman retaliated and beat the child with the stick. The child swung at Herman first. Herman beat him only after he was attacked. Several teachers witnessed the incident. Not one of us was asked to provide an account of the incident. Never take someone else's word against your child without asking questions!"

> *The LORD protects those of*
> *childlike faith; I was facing*
> *death, and then He saved me.*
> Psalm 116:6 NLT

Over the next few days, I did ask questions. I asked every child on our street that attended the school about the incident. It happened the way the teacher relayed it to me. Although I had never known Herman to start a fight, I had accepted the report. Influenced by my frustration, I had failed my child. I never made that mistake again. I was never quick to make assumptions.

No matter how many times that a particular behavior has occurred, it does not guarantee that is what happened in a different situation. Always ask questions. Keep an open mind. Ask open-ended questionsfollow-up questions. Look at every situation from an analytical viewpoint. Be willing to learn. Explore new ideas.

Create in me a clean heart, O
God; and renew a right
spirit within me.
Psalm 51:10

It is always dangerous to make assumptions and then proceed as if the assumptions are facts. Seek a second unbiased opinion. However, be careful in seeking that opinion. If possible, seek an unbiased professional opinion. When everything else has been tried, reevaluate your assumption. Don't get trapped by your assumptions. Don't get stuck at assumption junction.

Useless Excuses
Earline Hall

Why did I do such evil?
What was going through my head?
She looks a lot older than she is.
I was not the first man in her bed!

How could I have been so callous?
Why didn't I think of the cost?
I was feeling sad and lonely
drugs and alcohol were my boss.

Why did I betray a child's trust?
How did I let my family down?
I was trying to show some affection
I bought things when the parents weren't
around.

I don't have to answer your questions!
I am not really that bad.
I am not the only one who's done things.
The next time I babysit, you probably still
will be glad.

Lil' Earline

Useless Excuses

*For if you remain silent at this
time, relief and deliverance will
arise from another place but you
and your father's family will
perish. And who knows but that
you have come to the royal
position for such a time as this.*
Esther 4:14

A French Proverb states, "He, who excuses himself, accuses himself." As a child, my favorite Bible verse was, "In those days there was no king and every man did what was right in his own eyes." This scripture is repeated throughout the book of Judges. Today, we have kings, presidents, congress, senators, policemen, sheriffs, and judges. Yet, in many cases, every man continues to do what is right in his own eyes.

We all know what an excuse is. It is a reason to justify or explain taking an action or a lack of action. Useless excuses are those that do not benefit victims, children, or society. The word useless almost makes the excuses appear harmless and benign. The truth is excuses are harmful and allow the continuation of family violence, child molestation, incest, and rape. Most people making the excuses think that they are harmless and by their actions or inactions no harm or minimal harm is done. Initially, I was focused on the excuses that perpetrators make and through research for this book both formally and informally observations and on conversations. I made a startling discovery. Most perpetrators excuses are pretty absurd and easy to identify.

> *I say to myself, "The LORD is my inheritance; therefore, I will hope in Him!"*
> Lamentations 3:24 NLT

The most harmful excuses are made by society, family, friends, victims, child welfare staff, law enforcement, counselors, and even agencies that are charged to serve as advocates. When people who are responsible for ensuring a child's safety make excuses, additional people are placed at risk. This is not an attack on professionals in this field or the families. The truth is that there are many dedicated people who treat each victim with compassion and seek justice for the victims. They have a strong desire to ensure the perpetrator does not have access to additional victims. My concern is that justice and child safety is not consistent. It depends on many factors: the place where incident occurred, the place where the victim or perpetrator lives, the motivation of professionals that provide assistance, funding, and the case load sizes of those charged to assist families or protect society, community standards for ensuring child safety and the enforcement or tolerance of crime.

The greatest excuse for not being helpful, beneficial, and productive or supportive is simply no excuse, "I am not needed." This excuse can be used by anyone. Professionals can distance themselves or not get involved even when it is their job to assist. They can pass the responsibility on to someone else who works in the field. This person can refer you to someone else until you are shuffled around, worn out, and give up. If we do not assist those who need help, one day we may need assistance and find none.

Family and friends can be of assistance in supporting victims, accepting what has occurred, protecting child victims, assisting with investigations, providing preventive measures to ensure that all victims are recognized and treated, ensuring that the perpetrator does not have access to additional victims, or by not minimizing what has happened to the victim or others. Some family members will lie to protect perpetrators, attempt to discredit victims with personal attacks, and even blame innocent parties for the abuse. All too often, the next victim of a perpetrator is the person who protects the perpetrator or someone that is close to them.

Perpetrators make simple and idiotic excuses. Most molesters misrepresent their perversion. The following are some of the insane excuses that I have heard:

➢ He did not deny having sex with the girl but said it was consensual.

➢ A fifty-year-old man convicted of sexually assaulting a child, should not serve time because he's too short. The 5' 1'' molester will be doing probation instead, out of concern that other prisoners might pick on him.

➢ "I did not entice them. Neither did I possess a 'pedophilic predator's mind." However, he stated that he gave in after he saw them taking off their clothes. While taking a shower in his apartment after a soccer game, he saw the boys. When one of the boys was alone with him in his apartment, he asked the boy if he could perform oral sex on him.

> Those defending one molester stressed the incident only lasted a second or two. They said, "Isaac was extremely embarrassed by his actions which were deeply regretted."

> "Never did I force, coerce, or intimidate the boys I loved. I didn't have to."

> When one pedophile was asked, "Other than "wired wrong," are there any other reasons why men are sexually attracted to little girls? The pedophile couldn't even explain it; he asked, "Why are gay people gay?"

> It's just what he's attracted to: their innocence and their laugh.

> OTHERS just don't understand them, the depth of their love.

> "I had to plead guilty of the loving, affectionate sex-play I had with four boys to whom I had given a home."

➤ "I've never had sex with a boy I didn't first love."

➤ Why was a man, with a long history of criminal behavior, given such a lenient sentence for such a serious assault? "Well - Rashad had consumed far too much alcohol." He had been involved in a fight with his ex-girlfriend's brother, the court was told. He was given two-year supervised probation order.

➤ His "illness" was his sexual preference for men.

➤ A twenty-year-old man avoided a jail term after he begged a fifteen-year-old girl he had abducted to drop the charges against him. Because his mother was ill, his conviction would be hard on her. He was ordered to carry out 80 hours of unpaid work and to pay $200 in court costs.

➤ "It was only after two years, when the topic of sex was brought up by the boys, followed by the teasing and the verbal provocation that it started to happen. I never wanted this to happen in the first place."

Sacrificial Lamb

La'Toya Hall

Forgive them Father; they know not what

they've done

For if they knew, then they would surely run

My clothes are out; they're sittin there

casting lots

But My blood is dripping, even I see the

spots

They've got this crown of thorns sittin on

top of My head

They say, for the Son of God, I am sure is

close to dead

Father their priests talk to You through this

little slip

But on this day that veils about to rip

I'm hangin up here knowin I'll die today

But with My blood, their sins are washed

away

I'm doing this so they can come to You

170

So they can speak to You and seek the
gospel truth
Dad, I know that it all won't change today,
But let this spark start a fire, that's all I
pray
Dad, I know that Your power will never be
diminished
So just help 'em out, Lord
It is finished!

Sacrificial Lamb

*Get rid of the old "yeast" by
removing this wicked person
from among you... Christ, our
Passover Lamb, has been
sacrificed for us*
1 Corinthians 5:7 NLT

Jesus was the last sacrificial lamb. He was the perfect lamb. He was the lamb without spot or blemish. He was uniquely qualified to die an atoning death on the cross. After His death, there was no need for another sacrificial lamb. Why then are so many of our children being sacrificed?

In sexual abuse cases, common tactics for defense attorneys are to blame and seek to discredit those who take action to defend and protect the sexually abused child. A jury may be offended if the attorney attacks the child's character. It is more acceptable to discredit and destroy the character of the child's defenders. The mother may be the easiest target. They may claim that the mother is insane or neglectful of her responsibilities to protect her child. They may also claim that the mother has coached or coerced the child to make false allegations.

Some mothers have reported that they faced disbelief when they acted on their child's disclosure of sexual abuse. They also report that they have been disbelieved by those who evaluated the allegations including police officers and Child Protective Services. Some professional may overly identify with the accused. Sadly, molesters, rapist, and child abusers work in all professional arenas.

> *If I had the gift of prophecy, and if I understood all of God's secret plans and possessed all knowledge, and if I had such faith that I could move mountains but didn't love others, I would be nothing. If I gave everything I have to the poor and even sacrificed my body, I could boast about it; but if I didn't love others, I would have gained nothing.*
> 1 Corinthians 13:2-3 NLT

An eighty-four- year-old priest was convicted of molesting forty-seven girls. At the time of the attacks, the girls were reportedly between eight and fifteen years old. The molester is reportedly convinced that he's locked up because the forty-seven girls molested by him over the course of thirty years asked to be violated.

He stated, "They led me on with the intent of destroying me."

He reportedly stated, "These girls that came over there every day, they planned it. I could hear them talking and they'd come in and sit on a chair and their skirt would be up to their …? Well, it was kind of attracting."

When the school principal accused him of inappropriately touching the girls, the priest steered the blame to the principal and the little girls. "The principal … came over and accused me of touching them. I said, 'Why are they here? Aren't they supposed to stay in the schoolyard? Get them out of here!'"

Great is His faithfulness; His mercies begin afresh each day.
Lamentations 3:23

Due to his advanced age and health problems, he was only sentenced to three years in jail. His abuse of these girls spanned a minimum three decades, ten times the sentence.

One of his victims reported that she was

punished for telling a teacher about the molestation. As consequence for making her allegations, she states that she was repeatedly locked inside her school's supply closets. She was reportedly instructed to consider her sins during the time that she was locked in the closets.

He lifted me out of the pit of
despair, out of the mud
and the mire.
Psalm 40:2 NLT

Over the thirty-year period, several of the girls stated that they reported the abuse. Some of them reported being punished for making the allegations. They report being punished by family members for making claims of sexual assault. These little lambs were sacrificed to save the priest's reputation. Because of his abuse, approximately thirty lawsuits were filed.

Scapegoat
Herman Hall

I'm a decoy!

Need a decoy...

so you don't get caught?

Just point cha' finger at your scapegoat and

say it's their fault

I'm sick of all da' lies and tired of the game

Because when the smoke clears,

It's the scapegoat they blame

How can you keep lying to yourself with no

remorse or shame?

It's easy to get a long-term scapegoat to

blame.

Have you ever given someone your best and

they still were ungrateful?

Or tried your best to show love only to be
treated excessively hateful?

Ever been ridiculed and scorned to the point
where you resent all negativity and you
begin to hate jokes?
That comes with the territory when you're
the village scapegoat.

Scapegoat

*But Christ being come an high
priest of good things to come, by
a greater and more perfect
tabernacle, not made with
hands, that is to say, not of this
building, Neither by the blood of
goats and calves but by His own
blood He entered in once into the
holy place, having obtained
eternal redemption for us.*
Hebrews 9:11-12

In chapter 16 of Leviticus, God instructed Moses and Aaron to select two goats every year for an offering. One was to be used as a sin offering to atone for the sins and transgressions of the people. Once the goat was killed, the blood was to be sprinkled on the mercy seat of the Ark of the Covenant. There God would view the blood as a sin offering, have mercy on the people, and forgive their sin.

The high priest would then lay hands on the second goat, which was allowed to live. The priest would confess the sins of the people putting them on the head of the goat. The goat would then bare the blame for all the transgressions of the people and would be set free into the wilderness, where God would remember their sins no more. The goat became known as the scapegoat.

> *This High Priest of ours*
> *understands our weaknesses, for*
> *He faced all of the same testings*
> *we do, yet He did not sin. So let*
> *us come boldly to the throne of*
> *our gracious God. There we will*
> *receive His mercy, and we*
> *will find grace to help us*
> *when we need it most.*
> Hebrews 4:15-16 NLT

Christ came as the final and Great High Priest. He didn't come to offer the blood of goats and calves but His own blood. He entered the Most Holy Place. Finally, He made the final sacrifice. He provided eternal redemption.

According to the Mosaic Law, most things were purified with blood. Without the shedding of blood, there is no remission of sin. Christ was offered once to bear the sins of many.

> *Set your affection on things*
> *above, not on things on*

the earth.
Colossians 3:2

A scapegoat is a person or group made to bear the blame for others or to suffer in their place. People often look for someone else to blame for their problems. By attempting to transfer guilt to a scapegoat, feelings of guilt, blame, aggression, and suffering are transferred away from the perpetrator and their family. This may fulfill an unconscious desire to resolve or avoid such bad feelings. This is also known as the displacement of responsibility. They blame both the scapegoat and his supporters. This allows them to cope temporarily with the family's feelings of guilt and embarrassment. This is a temporary solution to the problem. Unless the truth is discovered, the abuser's family will always have doubts. They will always have the suspicion. They will always wonder if the accused will someday attempt to abuse one of their children or grandchildren or someone they really love.

"Come now, and let us reason together," Says the LORD, "Though your sins are like scarlet, They shall be as white as

snow; Though they are red like crimson, They shall be as wool.
Isaiah 1:18 NKJV

When David was accused of molesting a young child, his immediate family was unable to accept the severity of his deviant behavior. They had known for years that he had some problems. They had chosen to overlook the warning signs. They never sought treatment for him. On more than one occasion, his sister's friends complained about his harassment of them. At one point, they were concerned that David was receiving expensive gifts from a homosexual friend. There was concern that David had touched a younger male child inappropriately. However, when his family learned of the molestation, this was more than they wanted to accept. There had to be another answer. There had to be a scapegoat.

Darrell was the first person to be offered as the scapegoat. When the young victim refused to name Darrell as the perpetrator, David's sister needed another plan. She discussed with her mother. They wondered if the child's grandfather might have abused her. This person proved to be an unsuitable sacrifice. This caused them to settle on the original scapegoat.

*Beloved, if God so loved us, we
ought also to love one another.*
1 John 4:11

Darrell had a close relationship with the child. He loves the child, and the child loves him. Darrell also had a close relationship with David and his family. He was particularly close to David's mother. At least, that's what he thought. When he learned that he had been offered as the scapegoat he was crushed. Darrell had been devastated to learn of the molestation. This served to compound his hurt.

Families often look for someone else to blame when they learn that someone in their family is a child abuser. Scapegoating causes great anxiety and misery. Scapegoats are found in almost every social context. There are scapegoats in schools, on the playgrounds, in families, at work, at church, in small groups, and in large organizations.

The perpetrator's desire to displace and transfer responsibility away from him may be unconscious. He may believe his own lies. Self-deception is often associated with scapegoating. Scapegoaters are often insecure people with a desire to raise their own status by lowering the status of the scapegoat. This happened with David's family. There was already ongoing resentment and jealousy against Darrell's family. Darrell was living a carefree lifestyle. He wasn't working, and there were minor brushes with the law. He seemed to be the perfect scapegoat.

When Darrell's mother, Cheryl, learned that David was scheduled to take a polygraph test, she was relieved. Finally, the truth would come out! This wouldn't end the pain but maybe in time, the family would begin to heal. This hope didn't last long. Cheryl was aware that the results were inadmissible in court. After talking to several law-enforcement officers, she also learned the results were unreliable. Cheryl decided to do further research.

On March 3, 2009, this story appeared at http://www.wltz.com/news/local/40693797.html:

Columbus Police Officer Arrested in Connection to Bank Robbery, Released on Bail written by Maria Jones
The Columbus Police Officer accused of assisting a bank robbery suspect was released on bond, this afternoon...

Subsequent news articles related to this story revealed some disturbing information. During the hiring process, the officer passed a polygraph test. The officer has now been indicted for involvement in the robbery. The test was administered after the bank robbery.

According to http://dictionary.law.com, some habitual liars pass lie detector tests, and innocent, honest people fail them due to nervousness and other factors. However, law enforcement authorities usually believe the results, which occasionally exonerate (clear) a suspect. Since the results are sometimes unreliable, they are not admissible in a trial and may be ignored.

When Cheryl learned these facts, she was disappointed. Information on countermeasures to pass polygraphs was readily available. Since early childhood, David had been an admitted compulsive liar. The detective handling the case had previously made this statement to her, "We may have to wait for his next victim to come forward." She feared that the next victim would be a member of her family.

Recently, I saw a billboard that brought this message home. In huge letters, it read, "REPORT RAPE! Consider the next victim! I echo those sentiments. Report rape! Report child abuse! Report child molestation! Consider the next victim! The next victim may be your child, your grandchild, a parent, a sibling, a spouse, or someone that you love.

Don't allow scapegoating to continue. The inability to accept responsibility for one's actions is also a curse. To that curse I speak now:

To the curse of blame and scapegoating, I speak now. You have no place in this family. Not only is this family a royal priesthood and a holy generation, it is a responsible generation. People in this family will acknowledge their wrong. They will acknowledge their sin. They will seek forgiveness from those they have harmed. They will seek forgiveness from God. You have lost your place. You have lost your control. Blame and scapegoating no longer reside in this family.

Dreams, Hopes, Wishes

I often sit and stare at the world,

And dream dreams,

And hope hopes,

And wish wishes,

And lately,

I listen to a mellow song,

As it dances a beautiful dance for me,

But these moments,

These moments never,

Never seem to last too long,

For after the dreams, hopes, and
wishes,

And after the singing dancing melody,

And after you and me and a stolen moment
of happiness,

After a glimpse at the timeless Natural
Universe,

Comes the stark reality of today,

His ugly face
pressed firmly
against mine,
Washing away
wishes of
yesterday's
dreams,
Crumbling
hopes,
Destroying
wishes,
Yes it's too
late to turn
back now,
For it was only just,
A dream!

If Only . . .

Martha said to Jesus, "Lord, if only you had been here, my brother would not have died." When Mary arrived and saw Jesus, she fell at His feet and said, "Lord, if only you had been here, ..."
John 11:21, 32 NLT

It is so difficult to be right all the time! Along with the burden of always being right, it is nearly impossible to keep those "I told you so" remarks to a minimum. At times, it seems almost impossible. Even when I remind myself not to say it, it usually slips from my lips. Those of us who know how things ought to be done have a responsibility to everyone else. We make them miserable or we fix their problems. In either situation, we take ownership of their problems. They become dependent on our help. We can easily resent them for not assuming more responsibility for their problems. They resent us for knowing everything.

More than one person in my family depends on me. Indeed, I am known as "The Problem Solver." This is not a role that I necessarily like. I often wonder, who is supposed to help me with my problems? God is always there but sometimes you want a person to be there. It's nice to have someone to listen to your problems. Listening is the key. So many times rather than listening, we jump in with our solutions or advice. In the process, we fail to listen. We also maintain ownership for the person's problem.

I will ask the Father, and He will give you another Counselor, who will never leave you.
John 14:16 NLT

Child sexual abuse can be hard to detect. Keep the channels of communication open. Listen when people confide in you. Listen when your children talk to you. Listen! Supervise your children carefully. Be alert to signs that children are afraid of some people. Notice signs that the child is upset. Notice abrupt changes in the child's mood or disposition. Be alert to changes in the child's sleeping pattern. These behaviors could mean sexual abuse but they could also mean that something else is upsetting the child.

The fears of the wicked will all

*come true; so will the hopes of
the godly.*
Proverbs 10:24

In 2002, a man was convicted of repeatedly raping two of his daughters over a twenty-seven-year period. Before he was stopped, he impregnated them 19 times and fathered nine children by them. The man was sentenced to twenty-five concurrent life sentences.

Sometimes parents do a wonderful job protecting and educating their children and they are still sexually abused. Some parents do not do as well as others. Whatever the situation, dwelling on the "what if" or "if only" will only escalate the pain. It is more productive to seek professional Christian help for both the child and the parents. It is important to know that with the right help and intervention, children can learn to deal with being sexually abused. They can go on to live happy and productive lives.

*Devote
yourselves to prayer
with an alert mind and a
thankful heart.*
Colossians 4:2

Life is filled with lots of, "If only..." Life is filled with lots of, "I should have..." The past is often filled with regret. "I should have..." or "I would have..." are common responses to the things that we wish had never happened. Blaming ourselves for things that were out of our control only delays the healing process. We can only do the best that we can with the information that is available to us. I hope that we learn from past mistakes and use these experiences to help others.

Decent Decency

Molesters, please have decent decency
Won't you hear my heart's cry?
Why won't you confess?
You can help correct this terrible mess

Abusers, please have decent decency
Truthfulness can't you at least try
Don't you know, I'll do my best
To make this the last time you fail this test

What happened to decent decency?
Why can't you stop the lie?
God knows what you've done
You tried to destroy His innocent one

What happened to decent decency?
Why would you destroy your family tree?
Why destroy your family with lies?
Your lies have multiplied like flies

What happened to decent decency?
This is no false alarm!
You have caused so much harm!
When will the pain be gone?
For decent decency, take responsibility for
what you've done!

Why don't you have decent decency?
Confess to the harm that you've done?
You caused enough damage with what
you've done?
This just can't be fun!
From your responsibility will you continue
to run?
Don't make others pay for what you've
done!
Don't continue to destroy your family with
these lies.
Your victim still cries.
Your sins you should no longer deny.
Give decent decency a try!

Decent Decency

*Confess your sins to each other
and pray for each other so that
you may be healed. The earnest
prayer of a righteous person has
great power and produces
wonderful results.*
James 5:16 NLT

Families like to believe that their family ties are strong. They want to believe that they will present a united front against any opposition. They often believe that the bond is so strong that nothing could break it. They believe that in spite of difficulties and differences, the family unit will survive. This is exactly what I believed. That was before my family was changed forever. My assumptions may have been true before the family was violated. Then it happened. It happened in my family. The ugly monster of child molestation reared its head.

*Why am I discouraged? Why so
sad? I will put my hope in God! I
will praise Him again.*
Psalm 42:11 NLT

This monster tore at the very core of my family. The Word is sharper than any two-edged sword; it separates the marrow from the bone. Today, I'm convinced that child molestation has the same capabilities. It will try to destroy your very soul. It will challenge everything that you ever believed in. Those who have always stood firmly for truthfulness and righteousness will find themselves torn apart. As they seek to find a place of neutrality, they will quickly learn that place does not exist. When we choose to do nothing, we do something. We allow injustice, abuse, and victimization to reign. When we choose not to become part of the solution, we inadvertently become part of the problem.

> *But I am trusting You, O LORD,*
> *saying, "You are my God!" My*
> *future is in Your hands. Rescue*
> *me from those who hunt me*
> *down relentlessly.*
> Psalm 31:14-15

My question now is how do we prepare for the side effects? When an allegation of child molestation is made, it can be expected that the accused will deny the allegations. It can even be expected that the perpetrator's family will go into denial. The tension in the family can be expected. Family members will choose sides. Relationships may be temporarily damaged or destroyed permanently. Nevertheless, what happens when the family goes on the offensive? What happens when innocent people are blamed? What happens when innocent people are hurt?

When Cheryl chose to support a family member who had been sexually violated by another family member, she had no idea that her friend would suffer. Cheryl warned her friend that the family crisis might have adverse effects on her. Elaine was sure that she would be able to handle any attacks that came her way. Nevertheless, she had no idea how severe these attacks would be.

Those who wait on the LORD
will find new strength.
Isaiah 40:31

The attacks began almost immediately. They were personal and degrading. The attacks were public and openly hostile. As a Christian, Elaine was in a difficult position. Naturally, she wanted to defend herself. On more than one occasion, she yielded to that desire. This only aggravated the aggressor. The attacks became more intense and vulgar. They were also accompanied by threats. Eventually, Elaine began to keep quiet whenever the attacks ensued. Although she remained quiet, she wanted to defend and justify herself. Elaine began to feel that the life was being sucked out of her. She described it this way.

Struggling to recover from the pain, she said, "It was as if someone took a coffee stirrer and inserted it in my heart. Very slowly, they began to suck the life out of me. Because the hole in the stirrer was so small, it was extremely painful."

> *Let every soul be subject unto the higher powers. For there is no power but of God: the powers that be are ordained of God. Whosoever therefore resisteth the power, resisteth the ordinance of God: and they that resist shall receive to themselves damnation.*
> Romans 13:1-2

Elaine's abuser eventually confessed to mistreating her. Prayerfully, they can both begin to heal. The negative interactions between them could have potentially caused both of them long-term financial damage. Through mediation, this was avoided. This was a side effect of another person's action. Because the perpetrator refused to admit his guilt, innocent people continued to suffer.

My question then becomes to the molester, why don't you have decent decency. Why don't you confess to the harm that you have done? Haven't you caused enough damage with what you have already done? This just can't be fun! From your responsibility will you continue to run? Don't make others pay for what you've done! Don't continue to destroy your family with these lies. Your victim still cries. Please try decent decency. Your sins you should no longer deny.

Janet Ross faces more than twenty-five years in prison after being found guilty of one count each of first-degree kidnapping with sexual motivation, first-degree child molesting, and two counts of third-degree child rape. The thirty-three-year-old former elementary school teacher was convicted of having sex with a ten-year-old student and his fifteen-year-old brother.

The defense and the prosecution agreed to the facts in Patriot County Superior Court. Judge B.

Stallworth reviewed the facts and issued his ruling. Prosecutors say the former McCalheney Elementary School teacher abducted the ten-year-old student from his Talbot home. They drove for more than a hundred miles. She was accused of having sex with him at a highway rest area in 2007. They say that summer she also had sex with his fifteen-year-old brother.

Humble yourselves before God.
Resist the Devil, and he
will flee from you.
James 4:7 NLT

Telling the truth or confessing may be difficult but it can be done. When we think of our own selfish needs rather than the needs of others, it can be almost impossible. God is able to strengthen us in any situation.

When I faced incarceration years ago, I found myself in this same predicament. Fearful of losing my freedom, continuously, I searched for a Word from the Lord on my situation. The answers that I received weren't specific enough to ease my troubled and worried mind. More than once, a sincere Christian advised me to tell the truth when I went to court. This was not what I wanted to hear. I wasn't looking for justice. I wanted mercy. More than that, I wanted grace. I wanted what I didn't deserve. I wanted assurance that I would not have to pay for my crimes.

> *And now, dear brothers and sisters, one final thing. Fix your thoughts on what is true, and honorable, and right, and pure, and lovely, and admirable. Think about things that are excellent and worthy of praise.*
> Philippians 4:8 NLT

It didn't make sense to me that I should tell the truth. The truth was that I was guilty. What I wanted was a miracle. I wanted to be told that I wouldn't have to go prison. I informed my lawyer, no matter what happened, I wouldn't be able to testify. This wasn't consistent with what I had been told but this was as close as my fear would let me come to telling the truth. In my opinion, as long as I didn't lie, I was telling the truth. There was no understanding that God was giving me instructions to tell what had happened in the house that day, voluntarily.

At last everyone will say, "There

*truly is a reward for those who
live for God; surely there is a
God who judges justly
here on earth"*
Psalm 58:11 NLT

As grew closer to the time for my case to be
brought to court, it became increasingly obvious that
there would be no plea bargain. Weighing heavily in my
thoughts was, "Tell the truth!" Again, I reminded my
attorney that I wouldn't be able to testify. As the trial
progressed, each witness lied to suit his or her own
purposes. As all blame for the crimes was being placed
firmly on me, my lawyer told me that I would have to
testify.

*Better is the poor that walketh in
his integrity, than he that is
perverse in his lips, and is a fool.*
Proverbs 19:1

The thought of taking the stand was horrifying to
me, and it was extremely obvious. While on the witness
stand, I was so nervous that I began to pop chewing
gum and stutter profusely. In my thoughts were ringing,
"Tell the truth!" How could I tell the truth? Telling the
truth meant that I would have to face the consequences

for my actions. That was not what I wanted. Rather than consequences, I wanted grace and mercy. Nervously, I fumbled miserably throughout the testimony.

When I returned to sit next to my lawyer at the defense table, he leaned over and told me that I was the worst liar that he had ever seen. He said that I had sealed my own fate.

> *Humble yourselves under the mighty power of God, and at the right time He will lift you up in honor. Give all your worries and cares to God, for He cares about you*
> 1 Peter 5:6-7 NLT

My Aunt Bobbie had been in the courtroom with me. She encouraged me to leave town to avoid going to prison. I didn't want to run for the rest of my life. I decided that I would tough it out. Although the thought of going to prison was repulsive to me, I wouldn't run.

Truthfully, I think the judge unfairly influenced the jury. As he explained the sentence, he was the first person to "Tell the truth." He gave me a fifteen-year sentence for the possession of cocaine and ten years for the possession of marijuana. The sentences would run concurrently. He had given me an extreme sentence for petty charges. If only I had "Told the truth!" My sentence may have been something less severe.

> ### *A man's pride shall bring him low: but honour shall uphold the humble in spirit.*
> ### Proverbs 29:23

Today, I'm begging for molesters everywhere to do what I should have done. I'm praying that a spirit of decent decency will come forth all across the world. I'm praying that molesters everywhere will begin to confess to what they have done.

> *Dear God, I pray for molesters everywhere. Let them know that You still care. God, bring about a spirit of conviction now. Touch their hearts like never before. Let them know that if they will only come to You, You will forgive all the wrong that they have done. God, let them know that You died for them, too. Father, give them the spirit of decent decency that they will cause no further harm to Your littlest ones.*

Black Sheep, Black Sheep
Consolation from the throne

Black Sheep, Black Sheep...

Where have you been...?

Hiding with your lovers, hiding with your

friends...

Black Sheep, Black Sheep...

Where have you been...?

Don't you understand...?

I'm your everlasting friend...

Black Sheep, Black Sheep...

Why are you in so much pain...?

Black Sheep, Black Sheep...

Don't you understand...?

The king's heart is in My hand...

Black Sheep, Black Sheep...

Why have you lost hope...?

Black Sheep, Black Sheep...

Don't you understand...?

I can help you cope...

Black Sheep, Black Sheep...
Why do you cry...?
Black Sheep, Black Sheep...
Don't you understand...?
I'm here to dry your eyes...

Black Sheep, Black Sheep...
Why is your head down...?
Black Sheep, Black Sheep...
Don't you understand...?
I'm preparing your crown...

Black Sheep, Black Sheep...
Why are you looking for temporal gain...?
Black Sheep, Black Sheep...
Don't you understand...?
Life in Me is eternal gain...

Black Sheep, Black Sheep...
Why worry, why fret...
Black Sheep, Black Sheep...
Don't you understand...?
I know your name...
I engraved it in the palms of My hands...

Black Sheep, Black Sheep...
Why so much anguish and pain...
Black Sheep, Black Sheep...
Don't you understand...?
I understand rejection...
I understand pain...

Black Sheep, Black Sheep...
Give Me your pain...
Black Sheep, Black Sheep...
Don't you understand...?
You're the reason why I came...

Black Sheep, Black Sheep...
Won't you come home...?
Don't you understand...?
My arms are open wide...
I'm crying...
My child won't you come...

Black Sheep, Black Sheep...
Don't you understand...?
I want to be your shepherd...
As only I can...

Black Sheep, Black
Sheep...
There was never any
lack...
Black Sheep, Black
Sheep...
Don't you
understand...?
I was with you in
HELL...
My blood brought you
BACK!!!!

Black Sheep

*You have turned my mourning
into joyful dancing. You have
taken away my clothes of
mourning and clothed
me with joy.*
Psalm 30:11 NLT

For most of my life, I felt like a "Black Sheep." Whether real or imagined, I can no longer tell. Certainly, I lived a life that no parent would want for their child. Black sheep have their own unique ways of relating to the world. They want to be accepted for who they are. They want to be accepted for the way they are. They do very little to conform to the rules and regulations of the family or society. In the absence of family members who will accept their behavior, they often gravitate towards friends with similar behaviors.

It can be difficult for a family to accept the unorthodox behavior of the black sheep. They will seek to redefine and mold the black sheep into a more socially accepted model. Black sheep often view this as rejection. However, the family may have a desire to spare their loved one from the painful consequences that are associated with their negative choices. If there is no compromise or mediation, the black sheep will bare their pain for many years. The family will endure shame, disappointment, and embarrassment. The family may experience separation or isolation as side effects of their differences.

When we reject wise counsel, we make dangerous choices. Many of the negative choices that I made have had lasting consequences. It has been more than twenty years since I was convicted of a criminal offense. I even have a pardon from a former governor of Georgia. Yet, for many, I will always be deemed an ex-convict.

The stigma of a criminal history remains forever. When we foolishly chose a life of crime, we had no idea that someday, we would want something different. We had no idea that one day we would seek legal employment. We had no idea that we were destroying our reputation and our creditability. We had no idea that for some people a "Black Sheep" can never be transformed into a "White Sheep."

We all have issues. We all have failures. We all have gray areas in our life. We all need grace and mercy. Although we deserve justice, we beg for forgiveness. We beg not just for our punishment to be ended, mercy; we beg for what we do not deserve, grace. We beg for an opportunity to see our scarlet sins made white. Although many of us have accepted the scarlet tread of redemption, we continue to wear a scarlet letter. Because of the sacrifice that Jesus made, our sins have been forgiven. They have been covered under the blood. They have been washed away because we have accepted the sacrifice that Jesus made for us. Why then are we still treated as "Black Sheep?"

Patient endurance is what you need now, so you will continue to do God's will. Then you will receive all that He has promised.
Hebrews 10:36 NLT

When I think about the things that I have endured, the things that so many people have endured, and that so many little children are enduring, I am reminded of another mother. I am reminded of a mother who would have been considered a black sheep during her life. I am reminded of a mother that was raised in a place that could only be called a ghetto. There was no subsidized housing or a housing project available to her.

I am reminded of a mother who became pregnant out of wedlock, while attending church. She was the good little church girl that became pregnant. There was even speculation that one of the devout men of the church was responsible for her predicament. I am reminded of a mother that was subject to public embarrassment and scrutiny. I am reminded of a mother who almost lost her fiancé. She could have easily been accused of being an adulterer or a fornicator. She could have easily been stoned to death because of her apparent crime.

> *Don't worry about anything;*
> *instead, pray about everything.*
> *Tell God what you need, and*
> *thank Him for all He has done.*
> Philippians 4:6 NLT

I am reminded of a mother who bore her child into poverty. She didn't have the benefits of a welfare check or food stamps. There were no government-subsidized programs (WIC) to ensure that she had a proper prenatal diet. I am reminded of a mother who didn't have a Ginny Linn crib or pastel baby clothes. She didn't have name brand tennis shoes and designer clothes. I am reminded of a mother who didn't have a private suite available for her child's birth. There was no medical insurance. I am reminded of a mother who didn't have a private physician. There was no Medicaid program available to assist her.

And if she be not able to bring a lamb, then she shall bring two turtles, or two young pigeons; the one for the burnt offering, and the other for a sin offering: and the priest shall make an atonement for her, and she shall be clean.
Leviticus 12:8

I am reminded of a mother who couldn't pay large tithes. According to much of the prosperity doctrine, she would be accused of living beneath her privilege. Some would say the people of God should never suffer such poverty. Others would say, "How dare she come to church with such a meager offering?" There are those who would say, "The days of giving a pair of turtledoves, or two young pigeons for an offering are over! You need to bring God a decent offering when you to come to church! This line is only for those who can bring a lamb! Those who bring the lamb will receive a special prayer. I'm going to touch and agree that they receive a hundred-fold return for their offerings. Those of you that that have your lamb, hold it up high and line up in the center aisle." She was never able to stand in this line. Some may have said, "Surely, she's keeping God's tithe; her husband is a business man."

I am reminded of a mother who received a prophecy that she was going to suffer. There was no prophesying of a fine house or a new car. There was no promises of the wealth of the wicked being given to her. There was no prophesying that she would possess the five-fold ministry gifts. When she brought her child for dedication, she didn't have a fine suit with shoes, hat, and a purse to match. There was no expensive jewelry or hairstyle.

> *Direct your children onto the*
> *right path, and when they are*
> *older, they will not leave it.*
> Proverbs 22:6 NLT

I am reminded of a mother whose child was missing for three days. There was no "Amber Alert" to assist in locating her child. She could have easily been accused of being neglectful. It could have been said that she failed to discipline her child. Some may have even said that she was a poor excuse for a mother.

I am reminded of a mother who watched when her child was being talked about and rejected. I am reminded of a mother who watched her child being used for what he had to offer. They took her child's clothes and used them as a means of financial gain. They took advantage of her child.

"When you go through deep waters, I will be with you. When you go through rivers of difficulty, you will not drown. When you walk through the fire of oppression, you will not be burned up; the flames will not consume you."
Isaiah 43:2 NLT

I am reminded of a mother who watched her innocent child being jailed. I am reminded of a mother who watched while her child was beaten with whips. She watched as the flesh was torn from her child's body. I am reminded of a mother who watched her son struggling with the weight of His cross. I am reminded of a mother who watched when a thorn of crowns was forced on her son's head. I am reminded of a mother who watched when her son was mocked and scorned. They even spit upon Him. I am reminded of a mother who watched as her son was nailed to a cross. I am reminded of a mother who watched her son, an innocent man die. I am reminded of a mother who watched when her son died without her dreams for him being fulfilled. Some may have said, "She must have done something wrong. She should have taught that boy right from wrong. Whatever happened to his daddy? He probably ran off with another woman because he was tired of that child."

> *In the past you have encouraged many a troubled soul to trust in God; you have supported those who were weak. Your words have strengthened the fallen.*
> Job 4:3-4 NLT

When I think of the pain and suffering that so many mothers endure, it is Mary the mother of Jesus that comes to mind. Oh, what pain our savior's mother endured! Moreover, why did she endure so much pain? She was chosen by God to be the mother of His unspeakable gift, JESUS!

> *He that dwelleth in the secret*
> *place of the Most High shall*
> *abide under the shadow of the*
> *Almighty. I will say of the LORD,*
> *He is my refuge and my fortress:*
> *my God; in Him will I trust.*
> Psalm 91:1-2

Mary was part of a generation that was looking for a redeemer and a savior to come with a sword and shield revenging them of their enemies. She had accepted the promises of God. She had born the Promised Seed but now the promise was gone, without seeking vengeance on the enemies of Israel. Perhaps, Mary didn't understand. Perhaps she thought all of her sufferings had been in vain. Perhaps, there were days when Mary endured the pain and suffering of feeling like a "Black Sheep." Yet, she was blessed above all women.

> *Comfort ye, comfort ye my*
> *people, saith your God.*
> Isaiah 40:1

Because a mother who was a "Black Sheep" gave birth to a son who provided "The Scarlet Thread of Redemption," we have been made free from the curse of our sin. A "Black Sheep" gave birth to hope. A "Black Sheep" has given us hope.

We accept the hope that Jesus has provided to every "Black Sheep." We are ever so thankful that You love the unlovable. We are ever thankful that You have provided the grace and mercy that we need. We are thankful that You have given us a new name. You have given us a name that bears no shame. You have washed our scarlet sins white. You have set us free from the curse of death, hell, and the grave. Thank You for breaking the curse!

Green With Envy

Why is it that you pretend to hate me?

Is it that you really want to be like me?

Is it really that you envy me?

When I look into your eyes

I'm staring into green seas

Why do you idolize me?

Don't you see what I see?

Jesus is making me

When I look into your eyes

They are full of green lies

It's not because of a shadow that I cast

Darkness doesn't always last

In the darkness, you see the past

But in the light of day

Green your eyes continue to stay

Won't you walk in the light...

Where the future looks so bright?

There are no shadows in His sight
It's not really trendy
To have eyes green with envy

Jesus says, "Won't you follow Me?"
He wants to make you free
There'll be more for me to see
When I listen to your cries
They'll say, "No green with envy in these
eyes!"

Green With Envy

*Behold now, Thy servant hath
found grace in Thy sight, and
Thou hast magnified Thy mercy,
which Thou hast shewed unto
me in saving my life, and I
cannot escape to the mountain,
lest some evil
take me, and I die:*
Genesis 19:19

What happens when one family member is consumed with jealousy for another family member? How do you destroy that green-eyed monster? What happens when one sibling begins to hate the success of another? Is it possible to love someone and resent them at the same time? How does a younger sibling handle feelings of 'walking in the shadow' of an older sibling? What makes one

Earline & Herman

family member obsessed with thoughts of, 'what's in it

for me?' What makes one person a giver and another a taker? I would like to know the answers to these questions and many others. I have heard the excuses. I have heard the explanations. With all the explanations and all the excuses, I still come up empty. I don't understand these questions. These questions are posed because I don't have the answers to them.

> *Blessed are they which are persecuted for righteousness' sake: for theirs is the kingdom of heaven.*
> Matthew 5:10

One family member may harbor a deep animosity towards another. What brings about this type of resentment? It's quite simple! One person tries to be the best that they can be! Should someone lessen their efforts at success to allow someone else to feel more comfortable? This jealousy can occur even when there was no conscious intent to outshine the sibling. Can anyone give them the confidence or assurance that they need to overcome their resentment?

> *Pay careful attention to your own work, for then you will get the*

satisfaction of a job well done,
and you won't need to compare
yourself to anyone else.
For we are each responsible for
our own conduct.
Galatians 6:4-5 NLT

In the desire to have a NORMAL family, one family member may choose to ignore these feelings. They may hope good deeds will change the situation. On some level, they may learn to accept these feelings and to minimize them. Only Jesus is able to change this situation. While waiting for the feelings to change, it is necessary to do what is right. In some ways, attempts may be made to earn or buy the love of the jealous family member. It doesn't work. As years pass, the resentment may get stronger. At some point, it can become impossible to ignore envy and jealousy or pretend that it's normal. Realizing the extent of the resentment can cause immense pain. Yet, from this pain it is possible to recover! In my own life, the pain is already subsiding.

After they arrived at Capernaum
and settled in a house, Jesus
asked His disciples, "What were
you discussing out on the road?"

*But they didn't answer , because
they had been arguing about
which of them was the greatest.*
Mark 9:33-34 NLT

A thirteen-year-old boy is accused of masterminding the killing of his sixteen-year-old half-brother. Investigators said the thirteen-year-old looked up to his big brother. Nevertheless, he didn't want to share the family business - a major drug ring.

The seventh-grader allegedly recruited a twenty-year-old cousin and thirteen-year-old friend to murder his brother. In December 2008, the three allegedly stole $10,000 in cash from the elder brother, killed him, and burned his body. Afterward they went to a car dealership and bought a used car. The motives for these crimes were reported as jealousy and greed.

*"For I know the plans I have for
you," says the LORD. "They
are plans for good and not
for disaster, to give you
a future and a hope."*
Jeremiah 29:11 NLT

When those who are supposed to care for you, supposed to love you and have your best interest in their heart, instead, begrudge your accomplishments, it can be a painful experience. We can spend an immense amount of time trying to earn the acceptance or approval of others. You can't please people who aren't pleased with themselves.

Those who are closest to your heart have the ability to do you the most harm. They may harm you emotionally, spiritually, and even physically but they have no power over your soul. The future is in God's hands. If we allow others to control our emotions and reactions, we give them control over our lives.

> "A wise man is strong, yes, a man of knowledge increases strength; for by wise counsel you will wage your own war, and in a multitude of counselors there is safety."
> Proverbs 24:5

Sometimes, we find ourselves in circumstances that lead us to trust the opinion of others over our own. The Bible tells us that in the multitude of counselors, there is safety. It also tells us not to walk in the counsel of the ungodly. After receiving counsel, we have a decision to make. The responsibility for that decision will be mine. Therefore, with the leading of the Lord, I choose to make my own decisions. I refuse to allow another person to control or dictate my actions, my reactions, or responses. Without my consent, no one can speak for me. To those who become *green with envy*, we can say, "God bless you!" God holds our destiny. We can be everything that He has created us to be. No one has to be *green with envy*.

To the curse of envy and jealousy, I speak now. You have been cursed at very root. Your stronghold has been broken over this family. You will no longer destroy this family with that green-eyed monster that was created under the cloak of pride. Each member of this family will excel at what God has called them to be. Old wounds are healed and the rifts in this family have been repaired. Members are secure in what God has purposed in their life. As members put aside their own selfish desires, God is getting the glory. It doesn't matter what it looks like. All things are working for the good.

Bitter Victory

A Victim's Honest Feelings
Lyrical Payne

With all the jacked up, foul things you've
done to me
You used me till you were through with me
You left me sore, battered, and you bruised
me
You made me feel like that was all I was
meant to be
How could you have done that to me?
I thought we were a family.
I'm hurt mentally, physically, emotionally
I feel as if I'm dying, not just spiritually
What more could this evil world do to me?
Can everyone tell that I'm in pain, and
bleeding freely?
If they can, then why won't someone reach
out to me?
I'm walking alone in the dark; can someone
please shine a light for me?

I've forgotten the sounds of happiness, joy,
love, and peace.
Can someone please just call out to me?
I'm stumbling around in this world blind.
Can someone please just help me to see?
With all the ugliness in the world, can
someone help me find just a little bit of
beauty?
With all that monster did to me,
why wasn't someone there for me?
I'm struggling to get away, why won't
someone help me?
Even though I've matured, is it still so hard
to see the little kid in me?
Is it because you're all blind, do you only
see what you want to see?
Y'all say that I'm evil, y'all talk about me
Y'all hate me and say that I live sardonically
I know it's no excuse but maybe he did this
to me
I'm screaming for help, why won't anyone
hear me?

Can't you feel the little girl in me, tugging at
your knee?
You people tell me it's easy to find victory
But maybe it's not for everyone; maybe it's
not out there for me
I cried out for help, where's my victory?
I came forth with the truth, and still haven't
received
I went to the law; they were no help to me
Tell me who's gonna help me get my
victory?
Why are y'all protecting him, he's the bad
guy can't you see?
Why does he deserve to take my victory?
This just isn't fair, what about me?
Don't I deserve at least a little victory for
me?
Y'all say life isn't fair, just wait and see.
You're right; maybe I'll never get my
victory.

V-i-c-t-o-r-y

For I know the thoughts that I think toward you, saith the LORD, thoughts of peace, and not of evil, to give you an expected end.
Jeremiah 29:11

Victory

I had a choice
I decided to use my voice
I could keep silent
It was tempting to be violent

I could take a stand
I could hide, the way that he planned
I could hang my head in shame
I could look for someone else to blame

I could continue to cry
I could let this monster get by
I could blame me
I could ask Jesus to set me free
I could let this injustice be
But other victims needed me
I'm taking a stand
I'll even take the witness stand

I thought about this curse
It was something we couldn't nurse
When I began to pray
Jesus made a way

Jesus gave me perfect peace
He heard my sincere plea,
"Don't let evil destroy Your plan!
Under Your blood is where I stand!"

This curse won't destroy me
Jesus wouldn't let it be
I'm throwing up both my hands,
Jesus gave me the victory!

Victory

*How we thank God, who gives us
victory over sin and death
through Jesus Christ our Lord!*
1 Corinthians 15:57 NLT

We sang an old song. The song begins, "I've got victory over the enemy and the world can't do me no harm." When we truly have victory over the enemy, the world can't harm us. We say the words and we sing the words. When trials come, we easily forget the words.

Sometimes, the enemy is within us. We have attitudes, prejudices, family history, and generational curses that seek to destroy us from within. Others may forgive us but we find it hard to forgive ourselves. We carefully evaluate others but fail to evaluate ourselves. We have answers for everyone's problems but none for our own problems. When others think their scars or pain is invisible, we see every one of them. Yet, we hide from our own pain.

*Even if you are stained as red
as crimson, I can make you
as white as wool.*

Isaiah 1:18 NLT

If we are to obtain victory over the enemy, it begins on the inside. Every victory is obtained through courage. Every victory is obtained by overcoming obstacles. Every victory provides an opportunity for growth. Growth is often accompanied by pain. We reject growth because we have no desire to endure the pain.

I am humble and gentle, and you
will find rest for your souls.
Matthew 11:29 NLT

Another old song says, "Ask the Savior to help you. He'll go with you..." Our effort to recover from generational curses requires an honest and objective evaluation of the family of origin. While in college, I was required to write several papers that required evaluating family dynamics. This task was extremely difficult. At times, it seemed impossible. Sometimes, generational secrets or curses have become so hidden or engrained in a family that it is difficult to separate them from normalcy. As we tackle generational curses, God is willing to help us every step of the way.

Another song says, "Victory is mine! Victory today is mine. I told Satan get thee behind me! Victory today is mine!" We don't have to put off the recovery process. Victory can begin today! The curse can be broken today!

> *May our Lord Jesus Christ . . .*
> *comfort your hearts.*
> 2 Thessalonians 2:16-17 NLT

When the trials and circumstances in life seek to destroy us, we have an advocate with the Father. We have a savior who cares about the very hairs on our head. God is never too busy to hear our hearts cry. He wants to heal us from all the pain and devastation our past. He wants to give us an abundant life. Abundant life is a quality-filled life. God has a hope and a future waiting for those who trust in Him. We can cast our cares upon Him because He cares for us. He has given us a right to the tree of life. Today, that life can begin anew. We can be made free from every generational curse that seeks to destroy us. This is the day to say, "This curse stops here! It has been broken and it will never destroy my family!"

May you experience the love of Christ. . . . Then you will be filled with the fullness of life and power that comes from God.
Ephesians 3:19 NLT

The answer to breaking the curses over our lives is not in a magic potion or prescription. The answer is not found in fortunetellers, root workers, or false prophets. Jesus is the way, the truth, and the life. He is the answer. He always was the answer. He will always be the answer. Seek Him and live a curse free life!

Now the God of hope fill you with all joy and peace in believing, that ye may abound in hope, through the power of the Holy Ghost.
Romans 15:13

Additional Information

The following are some general guidelines for listening to children who have experienced sexual abuse.

- ➢ Sit on the same level with the child.
- ➢ Speak in a calm voice.
- ➢ Regulate eye contact: Don't stare or avoid the eyes, although in some cultures not looking into the eyes of others is a form of respect.
- ➢ Sit at a comfortable distance from the child
- ➢ Use the words the child uses, not only the slang but other words, too.
- ➢ Don't put words in the child's mouth.
- ➢ Be warm and accepting.
- ➢ Use simple, concrete language.
- ➢ Echo the last word of the child's statement
- ➢ Reflect back what you just heard to check to see if you heard correctly
- ➢ Use the 80/20 formula-adults do **only** 20% of the talking
- ➢ Repeat a key word
- ➢ Nod your head when you agree.

Polygraph Facts

Reliability

Numerous studies of polygraph validity have achieved rates of 80-95% for the kinds of tests used with specific issues, such as allegations in criminal cases. Drs. Heinz and Susanne Offe reported 93% accuracy in 2007 when using conventional field methods. In a 2008 article Drs. Frank Horvath and John Palmatier reported accuracy as high as 91%. Validity of polygraph remains controversial. Despite claims of 90% - 95% reliability, critics charge that rather than a "test", the method amounts to an inherently unstandardizable interrogation technique whose accuracy cannot be established. A 1997 survey of 421 psychologists estimated the test's average accuracy at about 61%, a little better than chance. Critics also argue that even given high estimates of the polygraph's accuracy a significant number of subjects (e.g. 10% given a 90% accuracy) will appear to be lying, and would unfairly suffer the consequences of "failing" the polygraph. In the 1998 Supreme Court case, *United States v. Scheffer*, the majority stated that "There is simply no consensus that polygraph evidence is reliable" and "Unlike other expert witnesses who testify about factual matters outside the jurors' knowledge, such as the analysis of fingerprints, ballistics, or DNA found at a crime scene, a polygraph expert can supply the jury only with another opinion..." In addition, in 2005 the 11th Circuit Court of Appeals stated, "polygraphs did not enjoy general acceptance from the scientific community". Charles Honts, a psychology professor at Boise State University, states that polygraph interrogations give a high rate of false positives on innocent people.

Polygraph tests have also been criticized for failing to trap known spies such as double agent Aldrich Ames, who passed two polygraph tests while spying for the Soviet Union. Other spies who passed the polygraph include Karl Koecher, Ana Belen Montes, and Leandro Aragoncillo. However, CIA spy Harold James Nicholson failed his polygraph examinations, which aroused suspicions that led to his eventual arrest. Polygraph examination and background checks failed to detect Nada Nadim Prouty, who was not a spy but was convicted for improperly obtaining US citizenship and using it to obtain a restricted position at the FBI.

Prolonged polygraph examinations are sometimes used as a tool by which confessions are extracted from a defendant, as in the case of Richard Miller, who was persuaded to confess largely by polygraph results combined with appeals from a religious leader.

Source:

http://en.wikipedia.org/wiki/Polygraph_examination

Some information contained in this book is adapted from Just in Case...Parental guidelines in case you are considering daycare and Parental guidelines in case your child might someday be a victim of sexual exploitation. National Center for Missing & Exploited Children.

Other Titles
By

Charlotte Russell Johnson

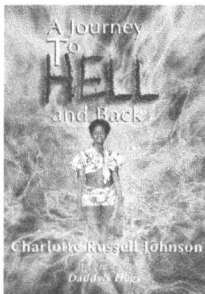

A Journey to Hell & Back
ISBN 0974189308

Daddy's Hugs
ISBN 0974189316

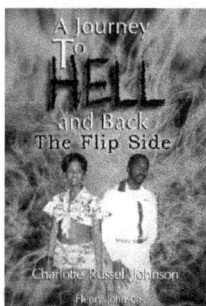

The Flip Side
ISBN 0974189324

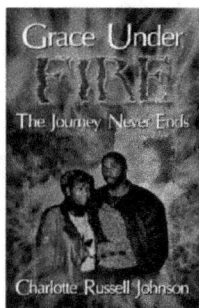

Grace Under Fire
ISBN 0974189332

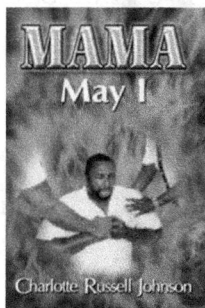

Mama May I
ISBN 0974179340

Mama's Pearls
ISBN 0974189359

Reaching Beyond, Inc.
www.charlotterjohnson.com

Helping hurting humanity to reach beyond the barriers
in their life, one barrier at a time.

ORDER FORM

Know someone else in crisis, or in need of
encouragement order additional copies of this book
to sow seeds of healing grace.

Postal Orders:

Reaching Beyond, Inc.
P. O. Box 12364
Columbus, GA 31917-2364
(706) 573-5942
Email us at: admin@charlotterjohnson.com
*Please send the following book(s). I understand that I
may return any book(s) for a full refund for any
reason, no questions asked.*

Qty.	Title	
_____	*A Journey to Hell and Back*	$14.95 each
_____	*The Flip Side*	$15.95 each
_____	*Daddy's Hugs*	$12.95 each
_____	*Grace Under Fire*	$14.95 each
_____	*Mama May I*	$14.95 each
_____	*Mama's Pearls*	$14.95 each

Sales tax:
   Please add 7% for books shipped to GA addresses.
Shipment:
   Book rate $3.50 for the first book and $1.50 for each
additional book.

Also available at www.charlotterjohnson.com

www.ingramcontent.com/pod-product-compliance
Lightning Source LLC
Chambersburg PA
CBHW060842280326
41934CB00007B/886